HIDDEN HISTORY *of* PONTE VEDRA

Maurice J. Robinson

The History Press

Published by The History Press
Charleston, SC 29403
www.historypress.net

Cover image: *Peaceful Lagoon*. Courtesy of Ellen Diamond and Fairfax Publishing.
ellendiamond.com.

First published 2012

Manufactured in the United States

ISBN 978.1.60949.815.3

Library of Congress CIP data applied for.

To Helen,
whose continued positive optimism and love made this possible.

Peaceful Inlet, by Ellen Diamond.

Ponte Vedra is replete with interesting people…who make up this wonderful, unusual bit of Heaven located on the northeastern coast of Florida.

—Gretchen Carpenter, Editor
Ponte Vedra Recorder, *November 1969*

Contents

Preface

After writing my first history book on Ponte Vedra Beach's history, I thought that it would be appropriate to continue with my additional research, including the many other significant historical events that have taken place throughout the years that never have been recorded in one document. With the many book talks and presentations I have given to those interested citizens of north Florida, I thought that the other significant events that have taken place should be recorded for those who live in this area and those visiting and wanting to learn more about the unique history of our area.

Indeed, many of those attending my presentations have asked about any other significant events that have happened in the Ponte Vedra's First Coast area. These many requests have encouraged and directed me to research and record other historical events, such as the African Diaspora to north Florida, Fort Mosé, South Ponte Vedra and other events that are unique to this small but historic area of north Florida.

It is still a unique privilege to me to attempt to put in writing many of the other significant events that have happened but were never recorded, all together in another history book.

Acknowledgements

I would, again, like to most importantly thank those at The History Press who have agreed with me that this additional history about our area needed to be recorded.

So many people in Ponte Vedra Beach have been so encouraging, asking about and providing me with other significant events and stories that have happened. I felt so enlightened by their requests and their historical information provided that I knew a second history book of this area of Florida had to be completed.

Again, my thanks need to be directed to Taryn Rodriguez-Boette, archivist, Beaches Area Historical Society (BAHS), for her encouragement, inviting me to make several presentations and having many of my books for sale at the BAHS. Many thanks goes to Janet Zimmerman, education coordinator and assistant manager of Guana Research Reserve, for her assistance in reviewing and editing my history of Guana.

There have been many others who have been so generous in sharing information about the many significant happenings in Ponte Vedra that I cannot name all of them.

Introduction

Ponte Vedra Beach in St. Johns County, Florida, survived in Guana from hundreds of years ago up to current events in recent times—making this a unique place to visit and live. My first book, *Ponte Vedra Beach: A History*, included and provided the history of many historic and unique happenings that only occurred in north Florida and did not happen in other portions of Florida or the South. I hope that this book will again spur your interest in the many unique events that have happened in our historic area of Florida.

For example, this small area of north Florida, above St. Augustine, has provided us with stories such as the significance of the Africans brought to the north Florida area as slaves—they eventually gained not only their freedom but also the freedom of other slaves in Virginia, North and South Carolina and Georgia who came to Florida's Fort Mosé. It has been very exciting for me to research the African Diaspora to north Florida and discover the many names that the white settlers called the African slaves and also the names that the slaves themselves called one another.

Our small area of Florida has seen history made in Guana and South Ponte Vedra, as well as history made via the Stockton families (beginning a tradition); the area also had the first unique retirement community. All of these stories and more are recorded here for your enjoyment.

GUANA'S HUMAN HABITATION

The Guana River Marsh Aquatic Preserve is more than 40,000 acres of sovereign submerged lands, including 12,415 acres of state conservation uplands. Conservation and Recreation Lands (CARL) purchased Guana. It is managed by the Florida Department of Environmental Protection as Guana Tolomato Matanzas National Estuarine Research Reserve (GTMNERR, 2,600 upland acres), Florida Fish and Wildlife Conservation Commission as Guana River Wildlife Management Area (GRWMA, 9,815 acres) and as Ponte Vedra Beach in St. Johns County, Florida.

A cross section of the barrier island from east to west within the park would reveal the following natural communities: Atlantic Ocean beach, sand dunes, coastal strand/scrub, estuarine river (fauna river) with associated salt marshes and tidal creeks, maritime hardwood hammock, freshwater depression marshes, pond pine flatwoods and shell mound forest.

GUANA—NORTHERN COMPONENT

Adjacent to and within the watershed of Guana River Marsh Aquatic Preserve (GRMAP) are significant public lands managed by various state and local agencies. Adjacent public lands include Guana River Wildlife Management Area (GRWMA), Deep Creek State Forest, Stokes Landing Conservation Area, Nocatee Preserve, Davis Park and a portion of the Twelve Mile Swamp Tract, including the Twelve Mile Swamp Wildlife Management Area and Conservation Area.[1]

Nocatee Preserve is a 2,400-acre parcel of salt marsh, floodplain forest and silviculture donated to St. Johns County by the PARC Corporation, developers of the town of Nocatee. The parcel was purchased to provide for the conservation of wildlife and passive recreation. The preserve is adjacent to

As the sun rises over the Atlantic Ocean, a new day arrives for those who enjoy a new beginning at Ponte Vedra Beach. *Photo by M. Robinson, 2010.*

the northwestern boundary of the GRMAP, providing three miles of natural shoreline and serving as a buffer to the developments of Nocatee.

Davis Park is a 138-acre county park located west of the GRMAP along County Road 210 (or Palm Valley Road). This park was developed for recreational activities and includes baseball, soccer, softball and football fields. The natural portions of the park include freshwater wetlands and pine silviculture.

Stokes Landing Conservation Area is 274 acres. The conservation area is located in St. Johns County, about three miles north of downtown St. Augustine. This area is open to the public for recreational activities such as hiking, bicycling, wildlife viewing and fishing.[2]

WILDLIFE

Many threatened or endangered wildlife species inhabit or spend part of their lives in this diverse collection of habitats. Marine mammals such as dolphins and whales, including the highly endangered northern right whale, can be seen from our beach. Three species of sea turtles, plus shorebirds like the least tern, nest

Residents fishing Ponte Vedra Lake on the old pier at Guana Park, 1940s. *Florida Memory, Division of Library & Information Services, Tallahassee, Florida.*

on the 4.2-mile undeveloped sandy beach. The reserve's magnificent thirty- to forty-foot-tall dunes host migrating peregrine falcons and the resident (recently reintroduced) Anastasia Island beach mouse.

Indigo snakes and gopher tortoises forage in the hammock, scrub and dunes. Forested areas, especially maritime hammock, provide critical nesting and feeding habitats for migratory songbirds, many of which are declining in numbers at alarming rates.

Finfish and shellfish, including blue crabs and large edible shrimp, inhabit the estuarine areas around Guana Dam. Wood storks, roseate spoonbills, brown and American white pelicans, wading and diving birds and waterfowl, as well as American alligators and river otters, are regularly seen in and around Guana Lake and the reserve's marshes and ponds. Ospreys and bald eagles soar overhead in their search for fish.

BEACHES

Recreational activities at GTM Research Reserve (officially designated on August 19, 1999)[3] are primarily based on the rich variety of resources found here (including the area along the beach) rather than on any man-made facilities.

There are no overnight camping facilities or developed picnic areas. There are three entrances to the beaches along the reserve for visitor parking, and then visitors can walk across A1A and enter the beaches area. The Guana Dam Use Area main entrance is open for fishing activities, and picnicking is certainly permitted anywhere in the reserve.

Guana's Past History

According to local history, reportedly twenty bundle burials were found in the center of the mound on the peninsula, along with twenty-five stone celts (excavated during the 1880s).[4]

The recovery of early pottery has been confirmed to be from the Guana shell ring—fiber-tempered pottery from the Orange period, or Late Archaic (2500–1000 BC), which has been collected from the surface of the site. (No excavations have been conducted.) It is believed that dwellings were located on the rings and that the central enclosed area was used as a community space and was kept relatively free of debris.

First Spanish Period (1565–1763)

Beginning with the white man's discovery of the Guana area, we find that Don Juan Ponce de Leon originally discovered this area after Columbus landed farther east in 1492. From his exploration of America, it is concluded that Ponce de Leon landed in 1513 on the Guana River lands. As we know, he only stayed one week before sailing south to the inlet at St. Augustine since he had no inlet at Guana for anchoring and protecting his ships.

When the Spanish arrived to inhabit St. Augustine in 1565, they established a system of missions that spread from St. Augustine westward to the Apalachicola River and northward into South Carolina. During the late 1620s, the Catholic mission town of La Natividad de Nuestra Señora de Tolomato, or Nuestra Señora de Guadalupe (Nativity of Our Lady of Tolomato), was located just under three leagues north of St. Augustine, placing it on the Guana Peninsula. The exact site of the mission remains unknown. The mission town was established to facilitate the passage of people and goods from St. Augustine to San Juan del Puerto (located today on Fort George Island). In 1689, some twenty-five families lived at the site.[5]

During the 1700s, the land held two Catholic missions, Santa Cruz and Santa Diego, the latter written about in histories of the Catholic missions as

Right: Sign posted at the Intracoastal entrance to Guana River Wildlife Management Area, Department of Environmental Protection Division of Forestry. *Photo by M. Robinson, 2006.*

Below: Roscoe Extension entrance sign, Guana River Wildlife Management Area, Fish and Wildlife Conservation Commission. *Photo by M. Robinson, 2006.*

the Church of the Palmettos. The Spanish mission Santa Cruz was visited by an Englishman, Jonathan Dickinson, a Quaker who was shipwrecked south of Hobe Sound and was given refuge during his odyssey to Charleston.

There was also a fort at what now is the GTM Research Reserve (formerly Guana River State Park). Guana, as it appeared on the De Brahm map of 1769, subsequently became the name that English speakers commonly applied to the area. The fort's name at Guana was "Nuestra Señora de Tolomato."

The Guana location was the second Tolomato site. The earlier town was located on the mainland of the Georgia coast. The Tolomato on Guana was probably destroyed during Carolina governor James Moore's attack of 1702 because it shows up in a third place, half a league from the presidio, sometime before 1711.[6]

Artifacts dating to the mid-seventeenth century were collected from the site, prompting John Goggin to tentatively identify Wright's Landing in 1925 as the likely location of the mission of Nuestra Señora de Guadalupe. Additional testing at the site in 1991 by the CARL Archaeological Survey and several members of the St. Augustine Archaeological Association (SAAA) indicated that intact mission period deposits exist in the wooded area of the site.[7] How much of the site remains is in question, as Wright's Landing has experienced severe erosion in the recent past.

The 1764 Moncrief map makes no mention of the abandoned mission, but it does list several place names on the Guana Peninsula: Alonzo Dias, Solio, Piripiri, Sto (Santo) Domingo and Sta (Santa) Ana. Alonzo Dias is in the general location of Wright's Landing. The relationship between the two places is not known at this time.

BRITISH PERIOD (1763–1784)

In 1780, a workforce of fifteen slaves was sent to the headwaters of the Guana River. The slaves were to clear one hundred acres of dry land and twenty acres of marsh in preparation of crop planting.[8] The former governor of east Florida, James Grant, owned the area. Dr. Daniel L. Schafer, of the University of North Florida, uncovered detailed maps of Grant's three holdings at the London Public Records Office. (Copies of the maps are now housed at the St. Augustine Historical Society Research Library.)

Governor Grant set the tone in 1763–64. He was an elitist by all reports—nearly feudal in his outlook. Three kinds of plantations actually came about: working plantations with on-site owners, working plantations managed by hired personnel and, lastly, parcels that were obtained for speculation only and never developed.[9]

To set an example, Grant established his own plantation on the outskirts of St. Augustine in February 1765. Located to the north, between the city gate and the remains of Fort Mosé, the three-hundred-acre plantation, known as Grant's Villa, became a successful indigo producer, employing between fifty and sixty slaves, with only one white overseer. For several years, "the Villa" served as an agricultural "college" to train the overseers of the province.[10]

Governor Grant continually stressed that good overseers were essential to profitable planting and that they deserved high salaries. While he advised that the overseers be white, he felt it mandatory that the laborers be black. "Africans are the only people to go to work in warm climates" was his constant credo.[11]

Grant's Villa was built entirely by slaves and spread across the peninsula and extended north, beginning at Alligator Point (previously called "Rogers' Point" or "The Point") located in the "Spanish Old Fields" (in Guana).[12]

The holdings maps show two areas on the Guana Peninsula: Mount Pleasant Plantation and Grant's Villa. (The third site, an experimental farm, is located north of the Fountain of Youth Park in St. Augustine.) Mount Pleasant Plantation was located at the northern end of the state lands, whereas Grant's Villa was located southward in the general area of Wright's Landing. The maps detail dwelling houses, offices, Negro houses, a stable, a smith's shop, indigo vats and a barn. In addition, the maps show the areas planted in rice and corn and those with orange groves. At Mount Pleasant Plantation, a system of dams and drains was built across the marsh to facilitate the movement and control of water into the fields.

In a story told by David Yeats (physician and council member) regarding a dispute with the Indians, one can see Governor Grant's show of respect for and fairness to the Indians in this area, as well as his ability to solve questionable disputes:

> *Some Indians being in town got drunk and forced their way into a private house in the night, raised a great riot, upon which the guard was called for and one of the Indians* [the Chehaw king's son] *was wounded and died two days after. Though the affair was purely accidental it is not known what turn it may take in the nation. To head off retaliatory violence when the Indian boy was killed in December 1768, Grant swiftly apprehended two white hunters. Comforting the father of the murdered boy in the Governor's House, Grant had the hunters arrested, tried and convicted, and with the father watching, had one of the men executed. Such acts strengthened a friendship with the Indians which would become extremely important during the American Revolution.*[13]

In 1782, "ninety acres of corn, twenty acres of rice and plenty of peas, sweet potatoes and other provisions had been planted: Four slave children were

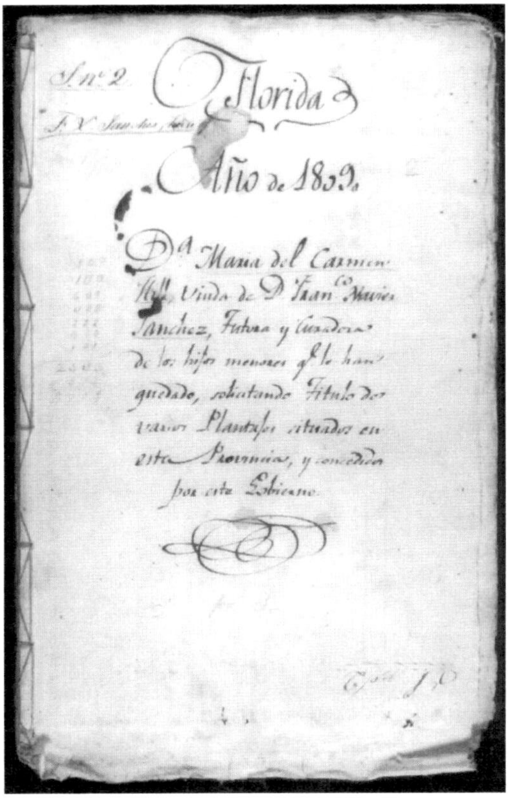

Deed of property transferred from the will of Francisco Xavier Sanchez, "Floridano Planter," to Maria del Carmen in 1809. *From* Spanish Land Grants in Florida, *1940.*

born at the plantation that same year.[14] Although Mount Pleasant prospered later (approximately 200 acres of rice, corn, peas and potatoes had been planted), the plantation and presumably Grant's Villa were abandoned when the Spanish again took control of Florida in 1783."

Places like Bay Gail Field, McNeill's Pond, Jencke's Landing, Cook's Pond and Hammock and Black Cook's on the Tolomato are evidence of inhabitants who occupied the Guana Peninsula during and after the influx of Minorcan farmers. A pond and Graveyard Road mark the location at Booth's Pond.

Raymond Road, with Wildcat Hammock at its end, backs up to Hammond Road. Still bearing southward and opposite Pine Island on the Tolomato River and Cotton Pond, Cappo Creek runs in near Cappo Road. Rock Landing is near the Little and Big Savannahs. Neck Road and the peninsula end at Shell Bluff and the coquina well, near the Savannahs, where Reeches Water Hole is located. Salt Run and a large Indian mound are situated where the Tolomato and Guana Rivers connect with the North River near St. Augustine.[15]

SECOND SPANISH PERIOD (1783–1821)

The next record of a homestead on the Guana Peninsula (Alligator Point) is the 118-acre "plantation" called Ostional Blanco, or White Oyster Shell Bank. The site probably was located at today's Shell Bluff. A 1793 survey of the rural parcels around St. Augustine reported that Minorcan homesteader Juan

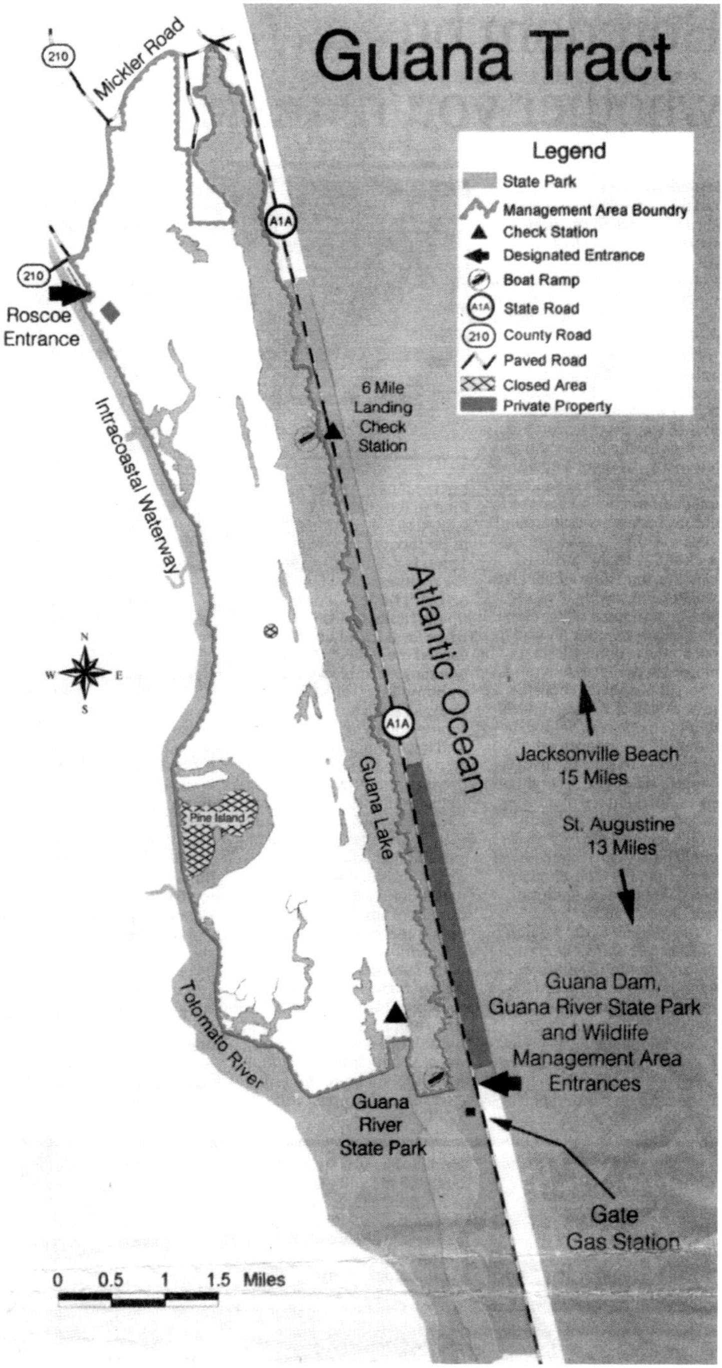

Aerial map of the entire Guana Tract from the Atlantic Ocean to the Intracoastal Waterway, *Ponte Vedra Shorelines*, January 25, 2003.

The many tall palm trees that beautify the Ponte Vedra area. *Photo by Ellen Diamond, 2012.*

Andreu, his wife and their six children and two slaves lived on the property. By 1804, there was a house, a kitchen and other smaller storage houses, as well as huts for the slaves. It is likely that the well was part of the Andreu homestead. Other Minorcans also lived on the peninsula, including Pedro Cosifacio, Lorenzo Capella, Juana Parades and Francisco Triay.[16]

The other plantations that followed and those at the "North River Settlements" of the North and Guana Rivers spread until private families were scattered along the entire peninsula. All of them farmed and struggled until none of their survivors remained on the peninsula. Eventually, it became mostly uninhabited.[17]

TERRITORIAL PERIOD AND STATEHOOD

At least one of the Guana plantations was for sale in 1823. The *East Florida Herald* (1823) lists for sale a 170-acre plantation on the east side of the North River, extending into Guana Creek. Included with the sale was 1 acre in the city that was cultivated as a garden with a variety of "choice fruits." The site was listed as being eight miles from St. Augustine.

A petition was filed in 1827 by Juan Andreu's widow regarding the fate of the Andreu Plantation—she wished to retain the plantation (the area around today's Shell Bluff) after Florida had become a U.S. territory. Congress confirmed this claim in 1827, and the land then belonged to her and the heirs of Juan Andreu as late as 1850.[18] This Spanish colonist at Guana changed his name from Juan Andreu to John Andrews. The coquina-shell well seen near the riverbank probably belonged to the Andrewses.

Project: Shell Bluff Landing site *(SJ32)*

Stabilization Issues: *Erosion due to tides, waves and wakes caused by boats*

Location: Shell Bluff Landing site is located along the eastern shoreline of the Tolomato River on the west side of the Guana River Peninsula in St. Johns County, Florida.

Site Description: The site is an extensive shell midden, containing materials dating from the Late Archaic Orange Period, the Florida Transitional Period, the St. Johns I & II periods, the 17th-century and early 19th-century Spanish occupations, and the American period, (ca. 2000 B.C. to the present). The site has been listed on the National Register since 1991.

Site Owner/Manager: The State of Florida owns the site, and the Department of Environmental Protection, Division of Recreation and Parks manages the site.

Contributing Organizations: Florida Department of State, Division of Historical Resources, Bureau of Archaeological Research; Department of Environmental Protection, Division of Recreation and Parks; Florida Department of Transportation; Army Corps of Engineers Waterways Experiment Station.

Management Problems: This site is threatened by coastal tidal fluctuation, wave action resulting from boat traffic and wind, and to some degree, the continuing rise in sea level.

Management Solutions: From 1984 to 1985 the Department of Environmental Protection (DEP), Division of Recreation and Parks, built a wooden bulkhead as a temporary measure to protect a 19th-century coquina well within the site, located on the river shore. In 1987, the U.S. Corps of Engineers Waterways Experiment Station initiated an erosion-monitoring project, in which the rate of erosion across the western face of the site was measured. In 1992, the DEP placed riprap and geo-webbing along the shoreline. To stabilize the shoreline, park staff are utilizing boulder riprap, which is occasionally renewed.

Storm-damaged bulkhead.

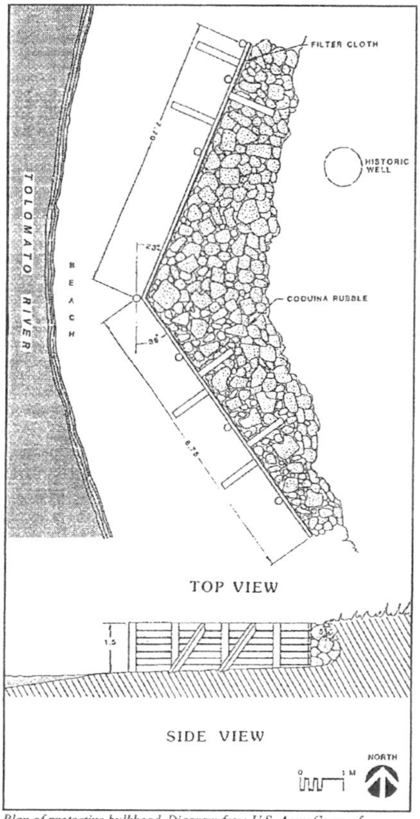

Plan of protective bulkhead. Diagram from U.S. Army Corps of Engineers Waterways Experiment Station 1990.

16 *Archaeological Stabilization Guide*

The Shell Bluff Landing Site is located along the eastern shoreline of the Tolomato River on the west side of the Guana Peninsula and is an extensive shell midden, containing material dating from the Late Archaic Orange Period, the Florida Transitional Period, the St. Johns I and II Periods, the seventeenth-century and early nineteenth-century Spanish occupations and the American period. *From the* Archaeological Stabilization Guide, *1992.*

The Dorr coastal survey map of 1860 showed a roadway beginning at Shell Bluff and leading north through the interior of the peninsula. Places identified on the Dorr map include Andrea (Andreu's homestead), Coopers Landing, Jenks Plantation and Mickler's Plantation. Several structures are also shown on the map. The sites have not been examined archaeologically, but it is likely that many of the plantation areas remain relatively undisturbed and can provide important information about nineteenth-century life. At least one cemetery, probably dating to the 1888 yellow fever epidemic, has been located on the Guana property, according to the St. Augustine Historical Society (SAHS). No markers are present, but it is believed that at least seven individuals are interred at the site.

The early 1900s brought changes to the character of the area. Along the northern portion of the Tolomato River, the Atlantic Intracoastal Waterway was extended through the use of canals. Extensive mosquito ditching in some of the salt marsh and interior wetlands was done on the Guana Peninsula. In the early 1900s, the National Lead Company owned the Guana property. The investment company Ponte Vedra Corporation/Stockton, Whatley, Davin & Company purchased acreage for a large number of different parcels at Guana from 1942 to 1980. Several plans for large-scale development were envisioned.

Timber harvesting began during the late 1930s and continued into the 1970s. A sawmill was located on the property during this period, and the sawdust pile can still be seen today on the northern portion of the property. The land was leased for cattle and hog grazing, apiary rights and a hunting preserve, as well as for a wildlife management area. The Guana Dam was created in 1957. It was designed "to increase and enhance habitat for wintering waterfowl in northeast Florida."[19] Other smaller dams and canals were also added in the hope of improving the hunting and fishing.

A less sophisticated but nevertheless effective impoundment dam had been built once before on the Guana River. That occurred in 1781 at Mount Pleasant Plantation and was accomplished by the enslaved black men and women owned by James Grant. The intention of the first dam builders had been to nurture rice plants with water from the reservoir.[20]

The Guana property was purchased by the Gate Petroleum Company in July 1983, and in July 1984, the State of Florida purchased the property for $49.6 million under the CARL program.

HISTORICAL/PREHISTORICAL CULTURAL SITES

Thirty-nine known significant Guana historic or prehistoric cultural sites have been located. Here are a few that are identifiable by location:

- Shell Bluff Landing Site
- extensive shell middens
- Wright's Landing Site
- Nativity of our Lady of Tolomato, a seventeenth-century Spanish mission
- prehistoric earthen burial mound
- A nineteenth-century Minorcan coquina block well
- Guana River Site, a shell midden site dating back to the Late Archaic Period (2500 BC)
- area south of Wrights Landing
- Jones Mound/Palm Valley, burial mound on west side
- Jenks Landing, shell midden on the west side
- Booth's Landing, east side of North River

Photo capturing an egret, horse and wild palms taken on the Stockton property, north of Guana Park. *Photo by Ellen Diamond, 2012.*

- Capo Creek, an undisturbed (shell) midden
- the old sawmill, northeast corner of the pond
- midden on the coast over the marsh, on the west side of Guana River (northeast corner)
- Little Orange Site, a shell midden located on the western shoreline of Guana River
- Guana River shell ring, a large midden one hundred meters in diameter
- There are twelve others sites where historical items have been found yet nothing remains to identify that particular area.

GUANA SUMMARY

As indicated, a total of thirty-nine culturally important prehistoric sites have been identified on the property, and it is likely that more will be found. The area is rich with history and nature, and it is open to the public. It has lots of history, nature and wildlife to offer.

AFRICAN NAMES AND THE AFRICAN DIASPORA TO NORTH FLORIDA

1500s

Slavery was practiced in Africa before the beginning of the Atlantic slave trade. Slavery and the slave trade were an integral part of African societies and states, which supplied the Arab world with slaves for centuries before the arrival of the Europeans. The African slave trade provided a large number of slaves to Europeans and their African agents.

In 1492, Pedro Alonzo Nino, African navigator of the *Santa Maria*, arrived with the explorer Christopher Columbus. African servants, slaves and explorers came to the Western Hemisphere with the first Spanish and French explorers. In 1501, the Spanish throne officially approved the use of enslaved Africans in the Americas.[21] Although Portugal was the first European country to engage in the African slave trade, it did not become one of the principal countries to realize great profits from the trade.[22]

Africans, from a pagan land and without exposure to the ethical ideals of Christianity, could be handled with more rigid methods of discipline and could be morally and spiritually degraded for the sake of stability on the plantation. In the long run, African slaves were actually cheaper. In a period when economic considerations were so vital, this was especially important. Negro slavery, then, became a fixed institution, a solution—and one of the most difficult New World problems.[23]

In 1672, the British king chartered the Royal African Company, the reorganized group that had held the monopoly for the past decade. For almost half a century, this company dominated the English slave trade and, indeed, became the most important single slave-trading group in the world.[24] The techniques of trading in slaves were developed after years of trial and error.

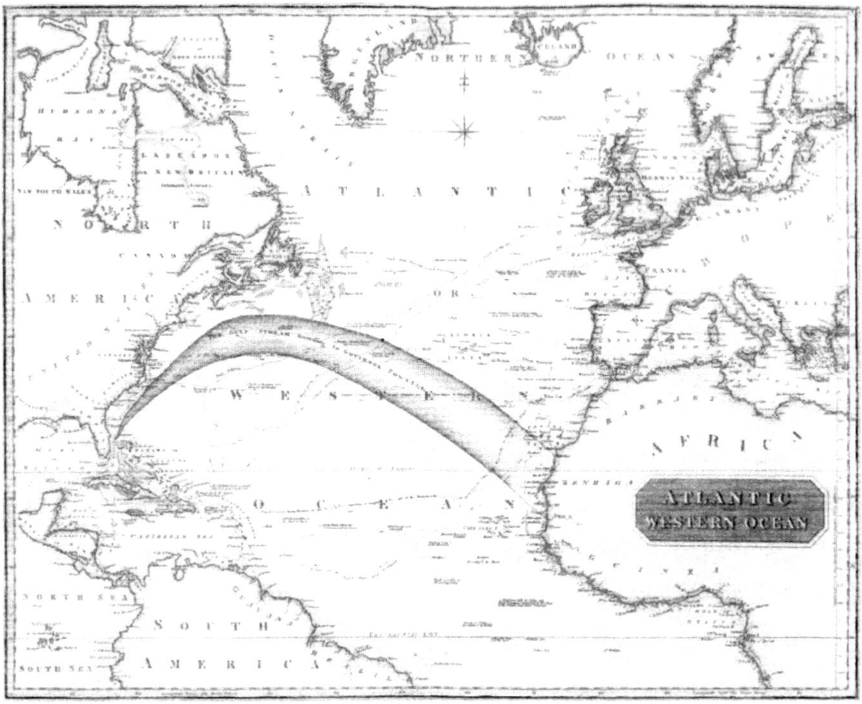

Map of the Atlantic slave trade and slave life in the Americas, 1815. Robert Sayer, *Atlantic or Western Ocean* (Edinburgh, 1815). Copy in the John Carter Brown Library at Brown University.

Perhaps not more than half of the slaves shipped from Africa ever became effective workers in the New World. The slave trade was still one of the most important sources of European wealth in the seventeenth and eighteenth centuries. It was not unusual for a ship to be compelled to call at four or five places in order to purchase as many as five hundred slaves.[25]

The vast majority of slaving was carried on in the area of West Africa, where civilization had reached its highest point on the continent with the possible exception of Egypt. In 1518, for example, the king of Spain granted a trader the right to ship four thousand Negroes to the Spanish islands. By 1540, the annual importation had reached about ten thousand. It must be remembered, moreover, that there was already developing an illicit trade, the size of which there was no way of determining.[26]

The following table lists the number of slaves (12.5 million) imported to six countries, with the United States importing the smallest number of Africans, other than the countries of the Denmark/Baltic category.[27]

THE TRANSATLANTIC SLAVE TRADE DATABASE
AFRICANS EMBARKING FROM 1501 TO 1866[28]

	Spain / Uruguay	Portugal / Brazil	Great Britain	Netherlands	United States	France	Denmark / Baltic	Totals
1501–25	6,363	7,000	0	0	0	0	0	13,363
1526–50	25,375	25,387	0	0	0	0	0	50,763
1551–75	28,167	31,089	1,685	0	0	66	0	61,007
1576–1600	60,056	90,715	237	1,365	0	0	0	152,373
1601–25	83,496	267,519	0	1,829	0	0	0	352,843
1626–50	44,313	201,609	33,695	31,729	824	1,827	1,053	315,050
1651–75	12,601	244,793	122,367	100,526	0	7,125	653	488,064
1676–1700	5,860	297,272	272,200	85,847	3,327	29,484	25,685	719,674
1701–25	0	474,447	410,597	73,816	3,277	120,939	5,833	1,088,909
1726–50	0	536,696	554,042	83,095	34,004	259,095	4,793	1,471,725
1751–75	4,239	528,693	832,047	132,330	84,580	325,918	17,508	1,925,314
1776–1800	6,415	673,167	748,612	40,773	67,443	433,061	39,199	2,008,670
1801–25	168,087	1,160,601	283,959	2,669	109,545	135,815	16,316	1,876,992
1826–50	400,728	1,299,969	0	357	1,850	68,074	0	1,770,979
1851–66	215,824	9,309	0	0	476	0	0	225,609
Totals	1,061,524	5,848,265	3,259,440	554,336	305,326	1,381,404	111,041	12,521,336

Note: About 16 million additional African slaves died after embarking to another continent.

During Florida's First Spanish Period (1565–1763), the Spanish used three types of enslaved workers. The first were Native Americans who served on Spanish *haciendas* (farms). The second were *ladinos*, skilled slaves brought from Spain who were allowed to work apart from their owners in exchange for payment under an arrangement called *jornal*. The third were African *bozales*, who performed heavy labor in fields and mines.[29]

The African American population of the north Florida area continued to increase during the First Spanish Period, when African-born slaves escaping plantations in Georgia and South Carolina came seeking asylum in Spanish territory. The Spanish offered two routes out of slavery: conversion to Roman Catholicism and military service in the Spanish army. So many blacks took advantage of this avenue that a company of black and mulatto militia was formed as early as 1658.

In the early years of the Spanish colonies, the slave trade was viewed as un-Christian and illegal. To overcome this dual disfavor, it was necessary for traders to secure special permission—the *asiento*—to bring slaves into the Spanish colonies. This made it relatively easy for the Crown to subject the traffic in slaves to rigid control.

The slave code in the South noted that slaves were not persons but property and that laws should protect the ownership of such property, as well as protect the whites against any dangers that might arise from the presence of large numbers of Negroes.[30]

The Spanish considered slavery to be an accidental and unnatural condition for humans. They did not believe that slavery was hereditary. Both the law of the Catholic Church and the Spanish legal code (the thirteenth-century *Siete Partidas* of King Alfonso X) treated slaves as humans rather than as property. The *Partidas* guaranteed protection of slaves from abusive masters or freeman and allowed slaves to testify in court against their masters. Additionally, because the Catholic Church treats marriage as a holy sacrament and views the family unit as sacred, slave owners could not split up a family by sale.[31]

Enterprising slaves were able to amass sufficient capital to purchase their freedom, especially if their masters were willing to cooperate. There are several examples of masters who set up programs of self-hire for slaves who looked toward purchasing themselves. Some slaves, regardless of their masters' attitudes, saved enough money to purchase their freedom.[32]

Escapes into Spanish Florida were among the earliest successful attempts at freedom and community, beginning near the end of the 1600s and concluding only with Andrew Jackson's march into Florida to eradicate the "Negro forts." In 1738, the Spanish governor of Florida offered freedom to British colonial slaves who escaped to St. Augustine. While Spain had long been part of the international slave trade and had used slave labor throughout its colonies, it disputed British claims to Georgia and South Carolina and wanted to keep those colonies as disrupted as possible. Encouraging runaways was a good way to do it. After the edict, slaves ran away in groups and individually to St. Augustine and nearby Florida villages.

Georgia advised its citizens to keep a sharp lookout for runaways from South Carolina on their way to Florida, and scout boats patrolled the water routes near the Georgia-Florida border. Many of the Florida villages consisted of the remnants of southeastern Indian tribes, gathered together for survival, who collectively became known as Seminoles.[33]

The Distribution of African Slaves in the Americas during the Atlantic Trade 1450-1870

North America	7%	
Central America and Belize		0.3%
Mexico		2.1%
Territory of the United States		**4.6%**
Caribbean Islands	43%	
Bahamas		0.2%
Bermuda		0.2%
British Virgin Islands		0.2%
Dominican Republic		0.3%
Dutch Antilies		0.3%
Trinidad & Tobago		0.3%
U.S. Virgin Islands		0.4%
Granada		0.8%
Puerto Rico		0.8%
St. Vincent, St. Lucia and Dominica		0.8%
Guadaloupe		3.1%
Leeward Islands		3.7%
Martinique		3.8%
Barbados		4.0%
Cuba		7.3%
Jamaica		7.8%
Haiti		9.0%
South America	50%	
Chile		0.2%
French Guiana		0.6%
Peru		1.1%
Argentina, Uruguay, Paraguay and Bolivia		1.2%
Venezuela		1.4%
Columbia, Panama and Equador		2.2%
Surinam and Guyana		5.1%
Brazil		38.2%

The distribution of African slaves in the Americas during the Atlantic Trade, 1450–1870, an image from Philip D. Curtin's 1969 work *The African Slave Trade: A Census.*

The transatlantic slave trade resulted in a vast and as yet still unknown loss of life for African captives both in and outside America. About 8 million Africans were killed during their storage, shipment and initial landing in the New World. The number of lives lost in the actual procurement of slaves remains a mystery but may equal or exceed the number actually enslaved. These figures would indicate the total number of deaths at about 16 million.

In the 1670s, it was noted that "Negroes or Indians, though baptised and enjoying their own freedom, shall be incapable of purchasing Christians, yet they are not deterred from buying any of their own nation."[34] A punishment was provided for loitering reunaways in the colony; for a second offense, a runaway was to be branded in the cheek with the letter "R."[35]

In 1790, the Negro population shifted with every passing decade, and this phenomenon alone was enough to indicate that the Negro population was among the most thriving of any of the ethnic groups in America.[36]

Medical Treatment of Slaves

In the antebellum literature, Africans were often referred to as "Negroes" or "niggers" and occasionally as "Ethiopes" or "blacks," and sometimes the African ethnic group was identified (Congo, Bambara and so on). Yet collectively, especially when referring to ships' cargoes, they were referred to as Africans ("salt water," "raw" or "fresh" Africans). The masses of enslaved people were of African descent. Many of those Africans who possessed significant European admixture (designated as mulatto, quadroon, octoroon or "white niggers") were also enslaved, not because of their European (white) blood or physical features, but ultimately because of their Africanity.[37]

Many studies provide the perspective of the medical doctors, particularly how they developed their practices and careers relying heavily on enslaved Africans as their subjects. The research represents the continued view of Africans as marginal beings in the white antebellum world. Africans did indeed serve as "guinea pigs" in the development of surgical procedures and were often subject to painful operations performed against their free will.

Surgery and experimental treatments/procedures were performed without the consent of the African. It was only necessary that the slave owner gave consent. The slave owner weighed the cost of medical care against the value of the enslaved African. Often physicians were called in too late to save the patient. A slave owner might surmise that his best alternative would be to forgo medical care and work the slave for the unknown number of years he or she had left. Some of these medical treatments were performed by veterinarians. The first African Americans to obtain professional degrees in veterinary medicine were Henry L. Stockton Sr. (Harvard School of Veterinary Medicine, 1889) and Augustus P. Lushington (University of Pennsylvania, 1897).[38]

Isabella Baumfree (Sojourner Truth), born in 1797 in Ulster County, New York, was the first black woman honored with a bust at the U.S. Capitol; she was first sold around the age of nine. In about 1827, Sojourner gained her independence from slavery. In 1874, after touring with her grandson, Sammy Banks, he fell ill, and she developed ulcers on her leg. Sammy died after an operation. She was successfully treated by Dr. Orville Guiteau, a veterinarian, and headed off on speaking tours again but had to return home due to illness once more.[39]

Before the Civil War, many hospitals in the southern United States treated both free and slave patients. A model was developed for the selective medical treatment of slaves. It is argued that the pecuniary benefits of hospital care increased with the price of the slave if healthy. Using a rich sample of admission records from New Orleans Touro Hospital, I found a positive correlation between the predicted price of the slave and the probability of hospital admission.[40]

When the practice of hands-on anatomical dissection became popular in United States medical education in the late eighteenth and early nineteeth centuries, demand for cadavers exceeded the supply. Slave bodies and thefts by grave robbers met this demand. Slave owners sold the bodies of their deceased chattel to medical schools for anatomic dissection. Stories of the "night doctors" buying and stealing bodies became part of African American folklore traditions.[41]

Bellevue Hospital, the oldest public hospital in the United States and a lineal descendant of an infirmary for slaves, accepted its first African American resident, Dr. Ubert Conrad Vincent, in 1918. This occurred at a time when many medical centers were not accepting African American residents.[42]

James McCune Smith (1813–1865)—first black American to obtain a medical degree, prominent abolitionist and suffragist, compassionate physician, prolific writer and public intellectual—has been relatively neglected by historians of medicine. No biography of Smith exists to this day, although he has been the subject of several essays. In 1837, Smith became the first black physician to publish articles in U.S. medical journals.[43]

American slave surgeon and "pioneer" gynecologist James Marion Sims became a highly prestigious figure in his later medical career, but the foundations of his success relied on the use of slave bodies and enslaved patients. In the slave South, the profession profited from the institution of slavery, and human experimentation and medical research were advanced specifically through the exploitation of the region's enslaved population.[44] Dr. Sims was an Alabama surgeon who carried out a series of experimental operations on black slave women between 1845 and 1849. Numerous modern authors have attacked Sims's medical ethics, arguing that he manipulated the institution of slavery to perform ethically unacceptable human experiments on powerless, unconsenting women.[45]

The historical experience of African Americans in our country has been shaped by the institution of slavery, dehumanization of blacks, segregation, pursuit of civil rights and racism in contemporary American society. Disparities in healthcare provide compelling evidence that issues of race or skin color for the descendants of slaves and other ethnic minorities persist in the twenty-first century.[46] At no time in history has the health of black Americans equaled that of white Americans. This distinction is particularly evident in the South, where blacks have been subjected to governmental policies promoting discrimination and segregation.[47]

Despite the legislation passed in the nineteenth century outlawing human slavery, it is more widespread today than at the conclusion of the Civil War. Modern human slavery, termed "human trafficking," comes in several forms. The most common type of human trafficking is sex trafficking, the sale of women and children into prostitution. Labor trafficking is the sale of men, women and children into hard labor for which they receive little or no compensation. Other forms of trafficking include child soldiering, war brides and organ removal.[48]

Racism in medicine, a problem with roots more than 2,500 years old, is a historical continuum that continuously affects African American health and the way that they receive healthcare. Racism is, at least in part, responsible for the fact that African Americans, ever since arriving as slaves, have had the worst healthcare, the worst health status and the worst health outcome of any racial or ethnic group in the United States.[49]

African slaves, however, had a natural immunity to certain diseases (including yellow fever and particular epidemics), and together with the climate and the nature of the work, this shaped the economic and social system of the area. Physicians offered all sorts of cures to deal with the medical problems of the area, and apothecaries also sold many nostrums, including leeches. Newspaper advertisements reveal that these bloodsuckers were extensively used for many decades.[50]

Members of the public were aware that graves were being robbed and countered with various protective measures. Since the deterrence of grave robbing took time and money, those elements of society that were least economically and socially advantaged were the most vulnerable. Enslaved and free African Americans, immigrants and the poor were frequently the targets of grave robbing.

The politically powerful tolerated this behavior except when it affected their own burial sites. Slave owners sold the bodies of their deceased chattel to medical schools for anatomic dissection. The physical and documentary evidence demonstrates the disproportionate use of the bodies of the poor, the black and the marginalized in furthering the medical education of white elites.[51]

FIRST AFRICANS GAIN THEIR FREEDOM

William Mayo Fulon's letterbook consists of letters written during his military service as captain of Company B in the Second Dragoons, later U.S. Riflemen. Most of the correspondence was written from various forts in Florida during the Second Seminole War (1815–43). While the majority of the letters focus on supply needs and personnel issues, some make reference to three African American guides and interpreters: Sampson, Sandy and Titus. Sampson and Sandy are among those listed as missing and presumed killed after the Indian attack on the trading post on the Caloosahatchee River on July 23, 1839.

There is some doubt in Fulton's letters as to whether Sandy was loyal or a traitor in collaboration with the Indians. The letters describe looking for Indian tracks and confusing them with Negro tracks. The letters voice suspicion that African Americans were trading with the Indians, and captured Indian women served as witnesses against Colonel Hanson's Negroes. Several letters testify to the employment of Titus as a guide and interpreter for the army and to the difficulty in procuring payment for his services. Captain Fulton was a resident of Richmond, Virginia, before and after his military service.[52]

Titus belonged to the Woodruffs estate and was an interpetor for the United States Army from 1837 to 1839.[53] The reference on July 23, 1839, listing Sandy and Sampson as missing and presumed killed also mentions eight others—six in the military and two citizens.[54]

It was the emancipated Christian slaves' belief that the Civil War and their emancipation were the direct consequences of their prayers. Some even argued that "the eleventh chaper of Daniel" had prophesied the war's coming and end.[55] African American men and women saw the Lord always at their side and were convinced that they indeed were His Chosen People. God was not only a personal friend but also an ally who supported their myraid modes of survival and resistance.

After Ponce de Leon landed in Florida in 1513, the Africans who came to the United States and Florida and their descendants were referred to and known by many different names, beginning with "Free Africans" and today "African Americans." In the African Diaspora to Florida, those who came to the South from their traditional homelands in Africa received/obtained many different titles, names and classification, as follows (years included where known):

ladino (1502–1518): a person of African descent who was Christian, Spanish speaking and acculturated from Spain; slaves brought from Spain who had been trained in a craft or as domestics.

black conquistadors (1510s): explorers of America who were awarded land grants and special recognitions; Juan Garrido and Juan Gonzalez (Ponce) de Leon were black conquistadors who crossed the Atlantic as freedmen in the 1510s; black conquistadors were present both as voluntary expeditionaries and as involuntary colonists.

Free Africans (1513): conquistadors who arrived on ships to America with Ponce de Leon heading to north Florida.

Africans (1525): the first transatlantic slave voyage traveled directly from Africa to the Americas; in the first two hundred years that blacks were in the United States, they commonly referred to themselves as "Africans."

maroons: from the word *marronage* or American/Spanish *Cimarron*; a "wild, savage, fugitive, runaway"; the man who was to become the first African American maroon arrived within a decade of Columbus's landfall on the very first slave ship to reach the Americas.[56]

esclavo: an enslaved person; people of all races and ethnicities could be enslaved, even Spaniards who were condemned to slavery for terrible crimes.

bozal/bocal: a person born in Africa (referring to a person who was not Spanish speaking, who was not Christian and was not acculturated to Spanish life); *bozales* performed heavy labor in field and mines; in the African context, *bocales* (Portuguese) or *bozales* (Spanish) were slaves imported from the interior to coastal trading sites.

African ethnic groups: the Spaniards were usually specific as to the ethnic group of the Africans living among them and would specify Congo, Banbara, Carabali, Madinga and so on.

blackamoor (circa 1540–50): slang for a black person or a dark-skinned person, especially from North Africa; unexplained variation of the phrase "black moor."

slaves (from the 1565 arrival of Menendez to 1865 at the end of the Civil War): the derivation of the word encapsulates a bit of European history and explains why the words "slave" and "slav" are so similar; they are, in fact, historically identical.[57]

person of color/people of color: terms used, primarily in the United States, to describe a nonwhite person or all nonwhite people. The historical term "free people of color" refers to people of African descent during slavery who lived in freedom.[58]

Creoloes/Criollos/Creole (1565 or later): could refer to Africans, Indians and Europeans born in the Americas as opposed to those brought from Africa; under the Adams-Onís Treaty, a Creole was any mixed-blood person with African ancestry; under Spanish Florida, such persons were free.[59]

mestizo (circa 1588–90): Spanish; a person of racially mixed ancestry, especially, in Latin America, of mixed American Indian and European (usually Spanish or Portuguese) ancestry or, in the Philippines, of mixed native and foreign ancestry.

moreno or Negro: persons of pure African heritage; mainly used in Brazil but also in America.

mulatto (1590): persons with one African and one European parent; a hybrid offspring.

griffe: a person of mixed Negro and American Indian blood; the offspring of a mulatto woman and a Negro; also, a mulatto.

negars: in 1619, the first African captives in America were described as "negars," which became the epithet still used by some today.

picaninny/piccaninny/pickaninny (1650): ethnic slur; offensive term for a black child.

sambo (1690–1748): "person of mixed blood in America and Asia" (1748), perhaps from Spanish *zambo* for "bandy-legged," from Latin *scambus* for "bow-legged" and from Greek *skambos*; name used variously in different regions to indicate some mixture of African, European and Indian blood; common senses were "child of black and Indian parentage" and "offspring of a black and a mulatto."[60]

hexadecaroon (1699): one-sixteenth black; an even less common term for the same ethnic mix; mestee, mustee or metisse were also used for a person with less than one-eighth black ancestry.

quadroon (1707): someone of one-quarter black ancestry—that is, with three white grandparents; also, a person of one-quarter Caucasian ancestry and three-quarters black ancestry; a quadroon can have a biracial/mulatto parent (black and white) and one white parent or black parent.[61]

First Freed Africans: in 1738, escaped slaves set up the Gracia Real de Santa Teresa de Mosé settlement near present-day St. Johns County in Florida, the first free-slave settlement in America; the second Fort Mosé was built just east of the original fort in 1782.

zambo, Spanish, or *cafuzo*, Portuguese (1748): someone with one African and one Indian parent; used in the Spanish empire and continues to be used today to identify individuals in Hispanic America who are of mixed African and Amerindian ancestry.[62]

Negroes, Negroid, Groid and Negress (circa 1763–1800s): named by the British; "Negro" means "black" in Spanish, Portuguese and ancient Italian, all of which derive from the niger (i.e. "black"); a term referring to people of black ancestry; in 1793, Spanish Florida was the only state remaining to legally import slaves (Negroes) from Africa; "Negress" was a word for a black woman or girl.

jigaboo, jiggabo, jijjiboo, zigabo, jig, jugg, jiggy, jigga, nigga, nigger, nigra, coon and spade: ethnic slurs; extremely offensive names for a black person; "only a black can call another black these names."

niglet: ethnic slur; a term used to describe a young black person.

free men of color (1770s): black soldiers served in this Spanish force, and some settled in Pensacola; also, as free men of color, some helped recapture British west Florida; a free person of color in the context of the history of slavery in the Americas is a person of full or partial African descent who was not enslaved, in the United States, such persons were referred to as "free Negroes," although many were of mixed race ("mulattos" in the terminology of the day).[63]

salt water, raw or fresh Africans (late 1700s to early 1800s): used, collectively, when referring to Africans in a ship's cargo.

wenches (1800s): a word degenerated through being used in reference to "young" slave women, especially those slaves with loose morals or a young, promiscuous servant woman.

colored/men of color (1800s–1960s): on February 12, 1909, the National Association for the Advancement of Colored People (NAACP) was founded; Lincoln's birthday in 1909 was a moment to take stock of the nation's progress since 1865.

children of color (1809): African American children taught in a white school in the evening in North Carolina and other southern states (parents of free people of color).

mammy (1830s): domestic servant of African descent; generally good-natured, often overweight and loud.

Jim Crow (1830s–1860s): a black person; also, the name for the segregation laws prevalent in much of the United States until the civil rights movement of the 1950s and 1960s.

house nigger (1840s): a derogatory term for affluent or highly educated African Americans; derived from the fact that African slaves who worked in the homes of their masters gained their favor and were able to advance socially by reporting suspicious slaves and/or their activity.

Miss Ann: a black woman who acts too much like a white one; while Miss Ann, also just plain Ann, is a derisive reference to the white woman, by extension it is applied to any black woman who puts on airs and tries to act like Miss Ann.

free-issue Negroes (1840s): offspring of white men and black women.[64]

quintroon (1842): a rarely used term that means a person of fifth-generation black ancestry. A quintroon has one parent who is an octoroon and one white parent.

blackie (mid-1800s): what visiting Charleston guests called black servants.

slang names (1860s): slaves were generally taught to treat elders with great reverence and to address them with honorific titles such as "Daddy" and "Maumer"; blacks of the same age group referred to one another as "Bro" (brother), "Titty" (sister), "Co" (cousin) or "Ma ma" (mother), which caused Northerners trying to discern actual blood ties no small confusion.[65]

contraband (1860s): Union term for runaway slaves; when referring to escaped slaves, it first entered the Official Records in U.S. Navy correspondence on August 10, 1861, when Acting Master William Budd of the gunboat USS *Resolute* used the term.

octoroon (1861): a person of fourth-generation black ancestry; genealogically, it means one-eighth black; typically, an octoroon has one great-grandparent who is of full African descent and seven great-grandparents who are not.

emancipated slaves: after slaves were emancipated in 1863, competitive wages fostered the invention of automation to replace the unskilled workers.[66] (This may come to define illegal immigrants in similar situations—twenty-first-century slaves.)

ape, buffie, crow, gable, mosshead, porch monkey, powder burn, quashie, sooty, spade, thicklips, nig-nog, nig jig and jungle bunny (1900s): ethnic slurs; mainly offensive terms for a black person.

Housing for the African Americans in Mineral City for the mining of chemicals on the beach, 1920s. *From the Beaches Area Historical Society Collection.*

tar-baby (1900s): a black child.

darky/darkie/darkey (1905–1910): ethnic slur; offensive term for a black person.

oreo (1910): a racial slur for being black on the outside and white on the inside, hinted by the appearance of an Oreo cookie.

Tom/Uncle Tom (1920s): ethnic slur; offensive and derogatory name for a black man who is abjectly servile and deferential to whites.

Uncle or Professor (1930s): since courtesy titles by whites were not used, it was permissible to call a favored black man "Uncle" or "Professor," a mixture of affection and mockery; he could never hear the words "Mister" or "Sir"; black women were "girls" until they were old enough to be called "Auntie."[67]

brownie (1940–1950s): a person of mixed white and black ancestry; a young, brown-skinned person.

nigras (1940s): a white person's term for inherently lazy and shiftless Negroes.

burr-headed nigra (1950s): having a head of straight hair cut very short (hence bristly).

nigger-lip (1950s): from an admonition that one must not suck the cigarette too far into the mouth and thus get the filter soggy.

blacks/black person (1960s–1980s): "Negro" superseded "colored" as the most polite terminology at a time when "black" was still generally regarded as negative.

Black Indians: people of African descent with or without significant Native American descent who were, or are, embedded with Native Americans or who possess strong cultural, social and political ties to their indigenous American heritage.[68]

African American or Afro American (1980s–present): characteristic of Americans of African ancestry; "Afro American culture"; "many black people prefer to be called African American or Afro American."

Florida emerged as second in black/African American population behind New York State. However, almost 20 percent of Florida's black population is foreign born. This is due to the huge influx of Haitians, Jamaicans, Dominicans and others of African descent from the Caribbean. Although they may be of Caribbean descent, several of the new emigrants are not coming from the islands. Many are moving from the Caribbean communities to big cities in the Northeast. They move here for the better weather without having to sacrifice culture. The decades-old trend of African Americans returning to the South has now extended to Florida in larger numbers.

Jonathan Dickinson's Journey through North Florida

1696

Jonathan Dickinson (1663–1722) was a Quaker merchant from Port Royal, Jamaica, who in 1696 was shipwrecked off the southeast coast of Florida along with his family and the other passengers and crew members of the ship. The party was held captive by Indians for several days and then was allowed to travel by small boat and on foot the 230 miles up the coast to St. Augustine.

The party was subjected to harassment and physical abuse at almost every step of the journey to St. Augustine. Five members of the party died from exposure and starvation on that journey. The Spanish authorities in St. Augustine, Ponte Vedra and north Florida treated the surviving members of the party well and sent them to find their northern passage.

Jonathan Dickinson's journal is a narrative written by a Quaker who was sailing from Jamaica to Philadelphia on the *Reformation* and was wrecked off Jupiter Island, Florida, near Jupiter Inlet. His departure on September 23, 1696, takes him, most of his party, his wife and his infant son on a journey, with the help of the Spanish officials, up the coast through St. Augustine, including stops in what is now Ponte Vedra and up northward in Philadelphia on April 1, 1697. The narrative of Dickinson's experience has direct interest for the historian in the glimpses it offers of Spain in Florida in the period when its power is declining yet it holds on tenaciously to what it had long ago established in that outpost of its American dominion. The documentation of that period is sparse, so far as printed works are concerned, whether in English or Spanish.[69]

So began an ordeal that would go on for forty-nine days as Dickinson and the others struggled up Florida's east coast. They managed to salvage a boat from the *Reformation*. It leaked, but it could hold five or six people. Part of the group—the injured, the weak and those who knew how to sail or paddle—went by boat along the coast. The others walked along the beach within sight of the boat.

For almost one month, they traveled like this, stopping when they could at Indian towns. By late October, as the weather was becoming chilly, exposure to cold had become a problem. At night, they slept in the open, with no coats or blankets to keep warm and no fire if it rained. It was hard to find food and fresh water, and everyone grew thin and sick. The land changed as well. They had to walk barefoot through marshes and swamps.

The long journey was especially hard on the women and children. On November 13, still two days away from safety in St. Augustine, people began to die. Benjamin Allen, a relative of Dickinson's, collapsed with fever and cold. Two male slaves, Jack and Cesar, and a female slave, Quanta, died from exposure. Hagar, another of the women among the slaves, carried the dead body of her young son until he could be buried. Dickinson's own wife, Mary, spent part of the journey trying to keep others on their feet, but she also had to carry and protect their baby boy. By the time the group finally stumbled into St. Augustine on November 15, everyone was close to dying.[70]

They stayed in St. Augustine from November 16 to November 29, 1696. After this, they were in Santa Cruces Indian Town (Guano area) until November 30, 1696. From that date until December 1, they were at a sentinel's house. For the first day or two of December, they were at St. Wan's Indian Town (now Duval County). Following are excerpts from Jonathan's journal.

The 29th of the Ninth Month, Being the First Day of the Week

(November 29–30, 1696)

Taking our departure from Augustine, we had about two or three leagues to an Indian town, called Sta. [Santa] *Cruces,*[71] *where, being landed, we were directed to the Indian warehouse: it was built round, having fifteen squares, and on each square a cabin built, and painted, which would hold two people, the house being about fifty feet in diameter; and in the middle of the top was a square opening about fifteen feet. This house as very clean, and fires being ready made nigh our cabin, the Spanish captain made choice of cabins for him and his folders, and appointed us our cabins. In this town they had a Friar, and a large house to worship in, with three bells; and the Indians go as constantly to their devotions, at all times and deafens, as any of the Spaniards. Night being come, and the time of their devotion over, the Friar came in, and many of the Indians, both men and women, and they had a dance, according to their way and custom. We had plenty of caffeena drink, and such victuals as the Indians had provided for us, some bringing corn boiled, others pease; some one thing, some another; of all which we had a good supper, and slept till morning.*

THE 30TH OF THE NINTH MONTH, BEING THE SECOND DAY OF THE WEEK

(Sentinel's house, November 30–December 1, 1696)

This morning early we left this town, having about two leagues to go with the canoes, and then we were to travel by land; but a cart was provided to carry our provisions and necessaries, in which those that could not travel were carried. We had about five leagues to a sentinel's house, where we lay all night, and next morning traveled along the sea-shore about four leagues to an inlet here we waited for canoes to come for us, to carry us about two miles, to a town called St. Wan's, an Indian Town on an island.

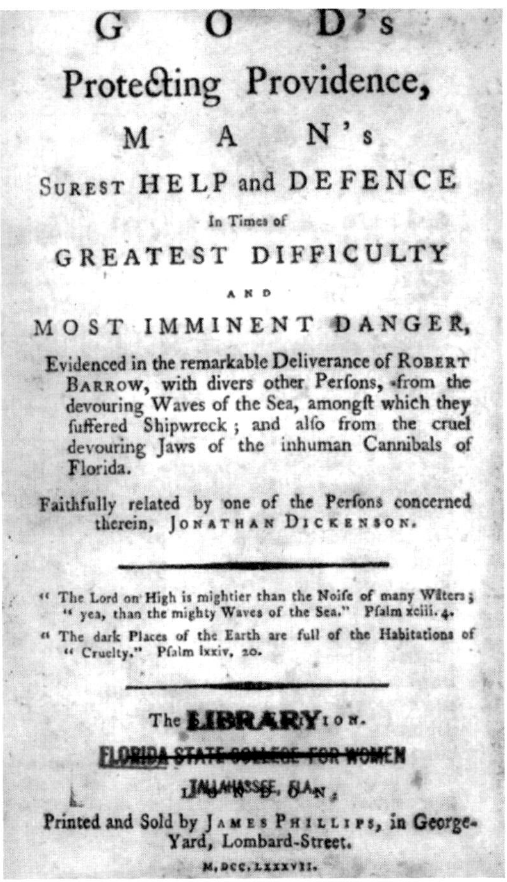

G O D's
Protecting Providence,
M A N's
SUREST HELP and DEFENCE
In Times of
GREATEST DIFFICULTY
AND
MOST IMMINENT DANGER,
Evidenced in the remarkable Deliverance of ROBERT BARROW, with divers other Persons, from the devouring Waves of the Sea, amongst which they suffered Shipwreck; and also from the cruel devouring Jaws of the inhuman Cannibals of Florida.

Faithfully related by one of the Persons concerned therein, JONATHAN DICKENSON.

" The Lord on High is mightier than the Noise of many Waters;
" yea, than the mighty Waves of the Sea." Psalm xciii. 4.

" The dark Places of the Earth are full of the Habitations of
" Cruelty." Psalm lxxiv. 20.

Printed and Sold by JAMES PHILLIPS, in George-Yard, Lombard-Street.
M.DCC.LXXXVII.

Image from Jonathan Dickinson's 1687 *God's Protecting Providence, Man's Surest Help and Defence in the Times of Greatest Difficulty and Most Imminent Danger.*

St. Wans Indian Town, December 1–2, 1696[72]

We went through a kirt of woods into the Indian plantations, for a mile. In the middle of this island is the town of St. Wans, a large town, and many people; they have a Friar, and a worship-house. The people are very industrious, having plenty of hogs and fowns, and large crops of corn, as we could tell by their corn-houses. The Indian brought us vidals, as at the last town.

Dickinson's arrival at St. Wan's Indian Town the following day was located in, now, Duval County on the east coast near the mouth of the St. Johns River. Dickinson and his party would continue their journal while writing his journal through what are now Georgia, South Carolina, North Carolina, District of Columbia and Maryland before finally arriving at Philadelphia, Pennsylvania, which was his party's original destination.[73]

Dickinson lived twenty-five more years, during which he became a wealthy business and political leader in Philadelphia. He filled numerous public offices, including chief justice of Pennsylvania colony and mayor of Philadelphia.[74]

Jonathan Dickinson's book of his exploits was published by the Society of Friends in 1687 as *God's Protecting Providence, Man's Surest Help and Defence in the Times of the Greatest Difficulty and Most Imminent Danger, Evidenced in the Remarkable Deliverance of Divers Persons, from the Devouring Waves of the Sea, Amongst which They Suffered Shipwreck. And Also, It Was from the More Cruelly Devouring Jaws of the Inhumane Cannibals of Florida, Faithfully Related by One of the Persons Concerned Therein, Jonathan Dickenson* [*sic*].

This book was reprinted sixteen times in English and three times each in Dutch and German between 1700 and 1869.

Fort Mosé

First Free African Fort

The story of Mosé begins in Africa and Europe, hundreds of years before the founding of America. By the 1700s, more than 1.5 million African people were brought unwillingly to the Americas as slaves. Many African cultures were present at Mosé, including Congo, Caravali, Mandingo, Mina, Guinea, Gambia and Arara. They also came from Cuba, Jamaica, Barbados, Antigua, Venezuela, Colombia and the Canary Islands.

Africans in Europe were gradually integrated into Christianity, even to the extent that it was possible to reach sainthood. Saint Maurice was a black saint popular in parts of Europe during the sixteenth century and was the patron saint of the Holy Roman Empire.

The first slaves in the Americas were not African, and the first Africans in the Americas were not slaves. The first black colonists were from Spain, and the first slaves were the Caribbean Indians enslaved by Columbus in 1495. It probably comes as a big surprise that when Pedro Menendez de Aviles established St. Augustine in 1565, he found persons of African descent remaining on the peninsula from earlier European expeditions.[75] The free black conquistador Juan Garrido arrived with Juan Ponce de Leon's expedition in 1513 after having served with other Africans in the earlier explorations and the conquest of Hispaniola and Puerto Rico.[76] The other African known to have arrived early on Florida soil was known as Estevanico, or Easteban. He was one of the survivors of the ill-fated expedition of Pánfilo de Narváez that touched the Florida coast in 1528.[77]

Earliest documentary evidence in St. Augustine dates from 1580, when fifty royal slaves were brought to the city to build and repair fortifications. By the seventeenth century, the Spanish Crown was responsible for supplying manpower to help build St. Augustine, and by the 1670s, there are records of slaves arriving from Havana to work at building the Castillo de San Marcos.

In 1686, the Spaniards in St. Augustine began to spread the word that escaped slaves would be given religious sanctuary in Spanish Florida. Africans in the English colonies seized this opportunity immediately. The first recorded group of fugitives arrived in St. Augustine in 1687 and included eight men, two women and a nursing child.[78]

During the Spanish control of Florida in the seventeenth and eighteenth centuries, a number of escaping slaves from the Carolinas and Georgia made their way south, determined to flee the oppressive conditions on plantations owned by the British or Americans. The Spanish had long used black slaves, beginning in 1565, to labor in Florida in both menial jobs and as servants to the wealthy Spanish.

Two miles north of St. Augustine, the Spanish established in 1738 a fort they called Gracia Real de Santa Teresa de Mosé,[79] what we call today Fort Mosé (usually pronounced "moh-*zay*"), the first free community of ex-slaves in North America. This was the first of two forts built in this area for the black community.[80] The settlement was officially known as El Pueblo de Gracia Real de Santa Teresa de Mosé. It was the first free African settlement in North America.

Fort Mosé, although legally sanctioned by the Spaniards in Florida, would have seemed like a Cimarron ("runaway") community to the English in South Carolina. Mosé was the slaves' symbol of hope. Mosé was established as a buffer against foreign encroachment and provided a third model of free black town formation.[81] About one hundred free black men, women and children lived at the fort, farmed the fields and helped defend St. Augustine from the British.[82]

Mosé was located at the head of Mosé Creek, a tributary of the North River with access to St. Augustine, and lay directly north of St. Augustine near trails running north to San Nicholas and west to Apalache. For all these reasons, it was strategically significant. Governor Montiano surely considered the benefits of a northern outpost against anticipated British attacks. And who better to serve as an advance warning system than grateful ex-slaves carrying Spanish arms? The freedmen understood their expected role, for in a declaration to the king, they vowed to be "the most cruel enemies of the English" and to risk their lives and spill their "last drop of blood in defense of the Great Crown of Spain and the Holy Faith."[83]

Perhaps the biggest mystery today about Fort Mosé is its pronunciation. Most historians prefer the pronunciation as "moh-*zay*." However, there are many others who prefer variations, such as "moo-sa," "mob-*say*," "moze," "mos" or "mo-sa." Anyone who has spoken the name has a strong opinion on the subject and is willing to explain at length why their pronunciation is accurate and all others are utter corruptions.[84]

Artist rendition of the reconstruction of Gracia Real de Santa Teresa de Mosé, or Second Fort Mosé (1753), located on the eastern edge of the marsh, consisting of captured or runaway slaves from the northern British colonies. *From St. Augustine's African American Heritage, "Black History," augustine.com/history/black_history/fort_mose, 2003.*

Established by Spanish Florida governor Manuel Montiano, Fort Mosé provided refuge for more than one hundred African fugitives fleeing from South Carolina to Spanish colonial territory. As Spanish Florida's first line of defense against the British colonies, Mosé represents a unique testimony to the courageous African Americans who risked their lives in the long struggle to achieve freedom.

The first group of slaves from Charleston and the English colonies fled from slavery and sought freedom in Florida. The first group to arrive in St. Augustine came in 1687 and included eleven men, women and children. King Charles II granted the runaway slaves in Florida their freedom in 1693. Governor Montiano granted the Fort Mosé land, two miles north of St. Augustine, for the runaways. In 1724, ten more runaway slaves reached St. Augustine, assisted by English-speaking Yamasee Indians. According to their settlements, they were aware that the Spanish king had offered freedom to those seeking baptism and conversion.[85]

There was a mission at Fort Mosé in 1728, Nuestra Señora del Rosario. Father Jose de Vellalba and Antonio Fernandez de Mora were in charge of the mission and fort.[86] Immediately, the men at Fort Mosé became members of the

Spanish militia and formed a free black company. In 1738, the captain of the Fort Mosé militia was Francisco Menendez, an escaped slave who had achieved the rank of captain in the St. Augustine militia. Menendez was a determined individual. Historical documents have revealed much about this remarkable man, a West African Mandingo by birth and former English slave who escaped to St. Augustine with the aid of the Yamasee Indians.

Freedom (for slaves), of course, came with a price. The occupants of the thirty-eight households at Fort Mosé not only had to become Catholics but also had to pledge to "shed their last drop in blood in defense of the Spanish Crown."[87]

The original fort was a small, twenty-meter-square enclosure containing a watchtower, a well and a guardhouse. With three walls made of earth, stakes and cactus, respectively, the fort was surrounded by a shallow moat and rested on a tidal creek to the east. Residents of Mosé came from diverse cultures in the Caribbean and West Africa, and their skilled labor, technology, music, ideas and traditions served as valuable resources to the Spanish residents of nearby St. Augustine.

On June 26, 1740, a force of Spanish regulars, dragoons, blacks, Indians, convicts and urban militia assaulted the English garrison at Fort Mosé. Out of 135 English at Mosé, only 24 were not killed or captured.[88] The soldiers and their families settled around these two forts, which were established throughout Mosé's twenty-five-year free African history. As one historian noted, "Fort Moosa…being about twenty miles from Fort Diego within two miles distance and in full sight of St. Augustine was made in the middle of a plantation for safety of the Negroes against Indians."

The Spanish allowed the blacks to settle there if they became Catholics. All of the inhabitants of Mosé were Catholic and received instruction in that faith. There was a church in the town, made of boards and thatch, as well as a resident missionary priest. The services were held in the St. Augustine cathedral.[89]

About one hundred free black men, women and children lived in the fort and helped the Spanish defend St. Augustine from the British, who wanted to capture the runaway slaves, take them back to their plantations and make them slaves again. Fort Mosé was destroyed in 1740 during the invasion led by General Oglethorpe of Georgia, but it was rebuilt several years later. During the twelve-year period between the destruction of the first fort and the construction of the second fort, the inhabitants of Fort Mosé lived in St. Augustine among the Spanish, Indian and other African residents of the town. When England took control of Florida in 1763, residents of Fort Mosé left with the Spaniards for Cuba, where they established a similar community in the province of Matanzas.

The situation of the slaves was somewhat different from that of other Florida locales because the St. Augustine whites permitted slaves to hire themselves out to fishermen, lumbermen and railroad builders. The slave owners kept most of the money the slaves earned from the practice but allowed the slaves to keep a small amount, which they used to support their own churches and clubs. The owners also allowed some of the slaves to live outside the master's residence in a separate part of St. Augustine; there the slaves had a freedom that encouraged them to express themselves.[90]

The second Fort Mosé[91] was built just east of the original fort in 1752 on the intracoastal waters. When the first Fort Mosé (1738) was destroyed, the Fort Mosé settlers lived inside St. Augustine until 1752, when their fort and town were rebuilt. The new site included a church, a house for a priest, a well, a lookout tower and twenty-two homes for the black families. The fort had three protected sides, while the side facing the river was open.

In 1759, sixty-seven African Americans lived at Fort Mosé: thirty-seven men, fifteen women, seven boys and eight girls. The former slaves at Fort Mosé knew the area well. They knew the plants that they could use as medicine, how to round up wild cattle and horses and where to find food. They were also good hunters and guides for the Spanish. The place had a large Catholic church where the people prayed, and a Catholic priest helped teach the people. They farmed for a living, but Native American attacks made that dangerous. The men also worked as carpenters and ironsmiths. The women grew vegetables, raised chickens and pigs and also baked, cooked, washed and sewed clothes. Like the Native Americans in the area, the people at Fort Mosé ate fish, turtles, raccoons, opossums and deer.[92]

The former free black settlers prospered there until 1763, when Florida was ceded to Britain by treaty, the end of the second Fort Mosé. The Fort Mosé African Americans evacuated with the other Spanish citizens to the northwest coast of Cuba. All of the inhabitants of the Spanish colony left their homes and sailed to Cuba, including the people of Mosé and the eighty-six Indians who lived in St. Augustine. Some of the Mosé residents settled in the Matanzas Province. Once in Cuba, they once again had to start a new life in an unfamiliar land.

Fort Mosé was refurbished by the English and was used as a fort during their twenty-year occupation of Florida. When the Spaniards returned in 1786, they also used Mosé as a military outpost. It was finally destroyed and abandoned in 1812. In that year, the fort was occupied by members of a group of American adventurers (known as the "Florida Patriots") who intended to capture Florida for the United States. They failed, and the fort was destroyed for the last time by the Spanish, African and Indian troops who routed the Patriots.[93] Not until eight decades later would the free black settlers' descendants be emancipated under the Thirteenth Amendment to the Constitution, free to start their own estates.[94] St. Augustine, which came under Union control in 1862, was one of the few places where Abraham Lincoln's Emancipation Proclamation actually took effect.

It wasn't until the 1960s that the fort was rediscovered. Today, there have been some excavations in the area where Fort Mosé was originally located. There is a sign on U.S. Route 1, just north of the St. Augustine city gates on Saratoga Boulevard, indicating the location for Fort Mosé that is east of U.S. Route 1. Now, more than 250 years later, the remains of Fort Mosé are as fragile as were the freedoms of its long-ago villagers. Time and tide have reduced Fort Mosé to remnant sections of ground-level shellstone foundations. Rising sea levels and dredging have turned the Mosé site into an island in the saltwater marsh.

Although there were other towns like Mosé in Latin America, it was the only example of a free black town in the colonial South. It provides an important, and heretofore unstudied, variant in the experience of African-born people in what was to become the United States.[95]

Historian Jane Landers, working with the unusually rich array of historical documents about Mosé, has been able to piece together the families who lived at Mosé. The religious records alone are recorded births, ethnic origins, naming patterns, godparent networks, deaths, records of epidemics and warfare and marriages. Intermarriage among native, black and white people was common throughout the Spanish New World, and elaborate systems of racial classification were developed based on the proportions of African, European and American Indian blood a person had.

Today, the Fort Mosé Historical Society is working to interpret this integral part of African American history and the brave heroes who helped define freedom before it was ever thought possible. The actual area where Fort Mosé once stood has been declared a National Historic Landmark. A fortress that housed runaway slaves seeking refuge from their imprisonment, Fort Mosé was the first of its kind in the New World. Fort Mosé will be a great memorial to how strongly those African Americans felt about freedom 250 years ago.[96]

This brief review of the possibilities for freedom and community life for blacks in Spanish Florida (Fort Mosé) demonstrates that African Americans created viable and vibrant free communities when circumstances permitted. It has been confirmed that African Americans exercised more important and varied roles in the colonial history of the Spanish frontiers of the United States than has previously been appreciated.[97]

It is interesting to compare the Mosé writings of Miss Irene A. Wright in 1924 with the Mosé writings in 1990 of Jane Landers. In 1924, Wright told us of the wealth of material found in the Archives of the Indies in Seville, Spain, pointing out that the material presents facts regarding not only the slave trade but also the valuable services rendered by the African slaves at Mosé.[98]

Fort Mosé Historic State Park Visitor Center. A short film and exhibits are available. Also, visitors can walk the boardwalk and view the sites where the two forts were built in 1738 and 1752 but later destroyed. *Photo by M. Robinson, 2008.*

In 1990, Landers used Wright's writing and translation of the original Spanish documents. Landers also added her extensive research and other historians' research to obtain a much more detailed description of the events that took place at Mosé.[99] These ethnohistorical studies make it clear that no history of Florida, or the Southeast, is complete without considering this complex and multidimensional African experience.[100]

Early Transportation in North Florida

1765 to present

Many realignments have taken place with various segments of Highway A1A. Built in the late 1920s as the Atlantic Coastal Highway, the road that now carries traffic from Duval County straight through Ponte Vedra Beach used to live up to its name, hugging the coastline along what is now known as Ponte Vedra Boulevard.

Joseph Charles Stehlin—manager of the National Lead Company's Buckman & Pritchard, later director of the Ponte Vedra Company and a man who helped name Ponte Vedra—was president of both the chamber of commerce and the Atlantic Coastal Highway Association in 1931. Highway A1A (Atlantic Coastal Highway) through Ponte Vedra was surfaced by B.B. McCormick & Sons and the State of Florida's chain gang, completing the surfacing in 1934. Stehlin clipped the ribbons that finally opened A1A through Ponte Vedra to St. Augustine.[101]

In the 1960s and '70s, A1A was altered. It was Grant Donaldson, "a remarkable, tenacious man," who came up with the idea to move the coastal highway to Ponce de Leon Boulevard or A1A, a twenty-foot-wide, county-owned "dirt cow path." The county did not know that Ponte Vedra existed, with only 1,400 people in both Ponte Vedra and Palm Valley. Local landowners Ponte Vedra Corporation and Eunice Pit Odom Semmes[102] donated the land needed, and the county finally agreed to build the road.

Years ago, the portion of the current A1A from Corona Road south to the present intersection with CR 210 was a portion of "Possum Trout" that included portions of Palm Valley Road, A1A and Corona Road headed to the beach. This was in the early 1900s. A portion of this road was also historically called "San Pablo Road," known to have been in use since at least the early nineteenth

The barge that was used to ferry people and cars over the Intracoastal in Palm Valley in 1934–35. *From the Beaches Area Historical Society Collection.*

century and probably in decades before that, as St. Augustine residents traveled to and from their cattle ranches in the Palm Valley area.[103]

Jim Stockton Jr. (Stockton Realty at that time) told Jacksonville mayor Haydon Burns, who was running for governor in 1964, "If you fund the bypass, I'll support you." Burns won the election, and funding was assigned. The coastal highway, by then known as State Road A1A, became a county road named Ponte Vedra Boulevard and the county's Ponce de Leon Boulevard became the state's new, two-lane A1A.

State Road A1A south of Mickler's Landing did not exist until the mid-1920s. In 1927, Mr. McCormick of B.B. McCormick Company personally established the alignment of the road from Mickler's Landing to Vilano Beach. The initial phase of McCormick's road building consisted of just grading the road with only men and mules from 1927 to 1930. The McCormick Road was finally completed in 1932; however, there were very few shacks that existed in this area now called South Ponte Vedra Beach.[104]

In addition to the 1960s shift to the former Ponce de Leon Boulevard in Ponte Vedra, A1A's path was reconfigured around the Serenata Beach development in South Ponte Vedra in 1980, around the Sawgrass Country Club and Sawgrass Beach Club developments and also around the expansion of parking and the rerouting at Mickler's Landing.[105]

Ponte Vedra's main road now through the area is A1A, which ran along the Ponte Vedra Boulevard until the bypass was built and completed in 1966. When the bypass was completed around Ponte Vedra Beach, the old road became SR203 (later CR 203) in St. Johns County and Duval County.[106] After the two-lane bypass road was built, it was later expanded to four lanes. It now has median strips that are landscaped with colorful bushy crepe myrtles and beautiful palm trees that parallel the coast from the northern entrance to Ponte Vedra Beach south to the Fairfield subdivision, just south of CR210. Highway A1A has the distinction of being the only Florida road (excluding interstate roadways) with a number and a letter in its name.

The bus used to transport passengers to and from Ponte Vedra Beach and the Jacksonville Beaches areas back in the 1920s. *From the Beaches Area Historical Society Collection.*

In 1945, State Road 1 was designated "Blue Star Memorial Highway" along its entire route through the state. The "Blue Star" was chosen to symbolize the memorial because it was used during World War II on flags and homes of families that had sons or daughters in the armed forces.

Apparently, there was great confusion in the name of the state road, which caused the State Highway Road Department (Department of Transportation) to change the name in 1946. Before 1946, the road was known as "State Road 1." Many travelers had constantly confused State Road 1 with U.S. Highway 1. Several complaints were received by the State Highway Road Department from St. Augustine residents about the two roads with practically the same name. A state law was passed in 1941 authorizing a renumbering; this didn't happen until 1945 because of the war. On June 11, 1945, Florida's state roads were renumbered.

The road was assigned the number SR 1 in the 1945 renumbering as the easternmost major north–south road. However, just across the Intracoastal Waterway, and in some cases on the same side, is U.S. Route 1 (SR 5), causing the confusion. The State Road Board changed the designation again to SR A1A on November 25, 1946, about a year and a half after the initial renumbering. SR A1A was finally designated for this north–south road.

In 1977, the secondary signs had the "S" (state) changed to "C" (county). Now, state roads are designated with SR for A1A, and county roads with CR include Ponte Vedra Boulevard (CR 203), Roscoe Boulevard (CR 210A) and Palm Valley Road (CR 210).

There is much difficulty in determining exactly what the "A"s stands for in the name. We can only speculate that the first "A" stands for the Atlantic Ocean and that the other "A" stands for an alternate route from Route 1 that runs from Maine to Florida. Of course, we know that the number "1" stands for the first easternmost highway along the Atlantic Ocean in Florida. The coastal road "A1A" in Florida actually starts at Fernandina Beach and follows the beach's route closest to the coast—that is, south to Miami Beach.[107] A1A now runs along Florida's East Coast Barrier Islands, separated from the mainland of the state by the Intracoastal Waterway.[108]

There have been many notable events that have happened on our A1A, with those involving the Whatelys being the most significant. The Brown Whately Interchange (Butler Boulevard and A1A) was named after Brown Whately, a founder of Stockton, Whately & Company, which developed Ponte Vedra Beach. He and his wife were killed in a car accident at the intersection in 1982 before the overpass was built in 1997.

NATURAL AND HISTORICAL FLORIDA HIGHWAY

The A1A Scenic and Historic Coastal Highway runs along this coastal barrier island, offering breathtaking views of the Atlantic Ocean and Intracoastal Waterway. It originates in north Florida at Fernandina Beach and extends to south Florida in Miami Beach. The unique geography greatly shaped the prehistoric and colonial history of the region. For centuries, the long estuary provided Native Americans with food and transportation. Later, the Europeans established seaside settlements, which became sites of commerce, culture and recreation. Today, the byway serves the same purpose, offering an abundance of culture, recreation and magnificent scenic views.

A Palm Valley postcard and letter from the Palm Valley Post Office that existed back in 1909 and 1932. Note that the postage rate increased from one cent to two cents. The Palm Valley Post Office was discontinued on April 30, 1932. *From* Florida Postal History Society, *Dean R. Briggs, journal editor, Winter Haven, Florida.*

The byway passes right through historic Florida locations such as Fernandina Beach, Jacksonville, Ponte Vedra, St. Augustine, Palm Coast, Daytona Beach, Cape Canaveral, Cocoa Beach, Melbourne Beach, Fort Pierce West Palm Beach, Fort Lauderdale and Miami Beach. All along the highway—and in numerous local, state and federal parks—the waters, beaches and coastal hammocks are clean, safe and accessible. The A1A scenic and historic coastal byway is, in essence, a scenic highway with authentic historical and recreational attractions and accommodations. It has been, and always will be, a primary coastal destination for travelers in Florida.

The A1A River and Sea Trail Scenic Highway still reflects many images of "Old Florida" that are rapidly becoming extinct and should be preserved.[109] The A1A Scenic and Historic Coastal Byway emphasizes the natural beauty of the route, the unique characteristics of its surrounding communities and the rich historic and archaeological resources. With these abundant resources, the quality of the journey along this scenic highway closely relates to the quality of life enjoyed by the residents and travelers alike.

HIGHWAY A1A TIMELINE IN PONTE VEDRA

1920s	State Road 1 or SR 1 (Atlantic Coast Highway) is opened; it is later called Ponte Vedra Boulevard and South Ponte Vedra Boulevard.

Building A1A from Mineral City (Ponte Vedra Beach) to St. Augustine. *From St. Augustine's African American Heritage, "Black History," augustine.com/history/black_history/fort_mose, 2003, and from the Beaches Area Historical Society Collection.*

1932	A1A is paved from Ponte Vedra Beach to Vilano Beach.
1945	It is designed as "Blue Star Memorial Highway."
November 25, 1946	SR A1A (Atlantic 1 Alternate), the A1A Scenic and Historic Coastal Byway, is completed with the new designation of A1A.
1947	It is rechristened as FL A1A.
1966	The bypass is opened and called Ponce de Leon Boulevard, or A1A in Ponte Vedra Beach proper.
1960s	Changes take place around the Sawgrass Beach Club development.
1980	It is reconfigured around the Serenata Beach development in South Ponte Vedra.

History of U.S. Highway 1 at Ponte Vedra

Dixie Highway in the Early 1900s

U.S. Route 1 today, on the western edge of Ponte Vedra, has been known by many names in the past. Some of these names and dates follow.

1765	Governor Grant collects five thousand guineas to build Old King's Road.
1776	Old King's Road, the northern route, is finally built by the British; it is also called Old Spanish Trail and Lone Star Trail (Jacksonville to St. Augustine).
1821	Sections of Old King's Road vanish into the muck.
1829	Congress decides to repair Old King's Road.
1880s	The Jacksonville, St. Augustine and Halifax River Railway (JSYAHRR), later taken over by the Florida East Coast Railway (FEC), parallel Old King's Road.
1914	John Anderson Highway is absorbed into the Dixie Highway.
1915–27	It becomes the Dixie Highway or Old Dixie Highway.
1935	It becomes U.S. Highway 1 or "Federal Highway"; the Dixie Highway is cosigned with Atlantic Highway the entire way.

Old King's Road / The King's Road

Old King's Road, which is the oldest commercial road in Florida, was built by British engineers in about 1776. With the advent of British rule, the need for settlers became acute. Colonel James Grant was appointed governor of east Florida in 1764 and immediately began to consider the construction of a road to unify coastal settlements and military installations, as well as to provide a conduit for settlers to repopulate the area. Lacking resources for the construction, the governor undertook the task of raising subscriptions to build the road and committed his own resources to the task. By 1765, Jonathan Bryan, a Georgia planter, had completed an initial survey for the northern portion, from the St. Mary's River to St. Augustine.

By July 1765, Governor Grant had raised five hundred guineas for the project and secured a pledge from the Georgia Colonial Assembly.

The initial plan was for a roadway that would run from Fort Barrington Georgia to St. Augustine. There was a simple (unnamed) roadway from Savannah, Georgia, to St. Augustine already existing:

> *By the summer of 1765 Georgia planter Jonathon Bryan searched for a route for the northern segment of the road between St. Augustine and the St. Mary's River. Riding on horseback for eleven hours, Bryan recorded a distance of thirty-eight miles from St. Augustine* [through Ponte Vedra] *to the narrows on the St. Johns River known as the Cowford* [now Jacksonville]. *Bryan predicted the "road must be causeway almost the whole way" with several short bridges, a project of "great difficulty."*

Coquina rock was first used to build Old King's Road. Coquina sedimentary rock is full of seashells from ancient ocean reefs and was mined in Flagler and St. Augustine as a building material. After being cut into shape, it would harden to form an almost indestructible building stone. The engineers building Old King's Road used large amounts of coquina for their causeways and bridges.[110] However, work proceeded slowly, and it was not until 1775, only months before the American Revolution, that the northern route was completed.[111]

According to a Historic Properties Survey, "The outbreak of rebellion in the thirteen colonies to the north dramatically altered the development of British Florida. Since the Florida colonies remained loyal to the crown, they attracted large numbers of loyalists investors and settlers who were seeking economic stability and political asylum."[112] So, during the American Revolution, Old King's Road still remained as the main pathway into Florida. St. Augustine was crowded with refugees trying to escape the conflict in the north, fearing the Rebel bands attacking, burning and destroying along the route.

Old King's Road was already half a century old in 1821 and was the only major road going south into Florida when the United States took over. While parts of it were in "tolerable state of repair," some sections had vanished entirely. Also in 1821, it was reported that sections had disappeared into the muck and palmetto palms. Bridges had been burned or destroyed, and sections of the roadway had been moved many times. After 1821, Old King's Road still saw a stream of wagons and new settlers moving south down this rough trail, often looking for new lands and fresh opportunities.

In 1829, Congress decided to repair Old King's and reextend it from Georgia to New Smyrna. The few local residents asked that the "old road made by the English Government, may be repaired and bridges built over the several small streams, which it intersects in its course. The road way had been in terrible condition, bridges gone, and sections had actually vanished."[113]

Old Brick Dixie Highway, now Route 1, built in 1916. *Polk County Historical and Genealogical Library, U.S. National Register of Historical Places, #05000311.*

The John Anderson Highway

The John Anderson Highway connected Miami, Florida, to Jacksonville, Florida. It was absorbed into the longer Dixie Highway in about 1915.

Dixie Highway/Old Dixie Highway

This road was cosigned with Dixie Highway (East) and Atlantic Coastal Highway (South) the entire length; the Old Spanish Trail and Lone Star Trail ran from Jacksonville to St. Augustine.

The name "Dixie Highway" persists in various locations along its route where the main flow of long-distance traffic has been rerouted to more modern highways and the old Dixie Highway remains as a local road. In some Florida cities, Dixie Highway (or sometimes Old Dixie Highway) parallels "Federal Highway" (U.S. Route 1), sometimes just a block away.

The Dixie Highway was a United States automobile highway, first planned in 1914 to connect the Midwest to the South. It was part of the National Auto Trail system (in the early part of the twentieth century) and grew out of an earlier Miami–Montreal highway. The final result is better understood as a small network of interconnected paved roads rather than as a single highway. It was constructed and expanded from 1915 to 1927.

The Dixie Highway was inspired by the example of the slightly earlier Lincoln Highway. The prime booster of both projects was promoter and businessman Carl G. Fisher, an American automotive and real estate entrepreneur. It was overseen by the Dixie Highway Association and funded by a group of individuals, businesses and local and state governments. In the early years, the federal goverment played a small role, but from the early 1920s onward, it provided increasing funding until 1927, when the Dixie Highway Association was disbanded and the highway was taken over as part of the United States Highway System, with some portions becoming state roads.[114]

The route of the Dixie Highway was marked by a red stripe with the letters "DH" on it, usually with a white stripe above and below. This was commonly painted on telephone and telegraph poles along the route. The eastern portion from Jacksonville, Florida, running south through Ponte Vedra and St. Johns County was largely replaced with U.S. Route 1.

In some of these cities and towns, Dixie Highway is the north–south axis of the street numbering system, although its diagonal route (not quite straight north–south) makes it not quite the best choice for this use.

Several likely old alignments exist here. One is east of the current road, just north of the St. Augustine Airport. Farther north, a road lies east of the current road; it may not have ever been paved but may have been part of the even older King's Road.

Before the U.S. numbered highway system was established in 1926, interstate traffic followed paths blazed and promoted by various trails associations, a system collectively known as Auto Trails. The system relied on dues paid by members along the route to pay for advertising. Improvement of the route was left to locals. The markers used were as colorful as some of the promoters. All you really needed to run an auto trail was a few buckets of paint and a knack for self-promotion.[115]

The United States Congress approved a plan for numbering all major roads in the country in 1926.

Shore Sawmill area or Cracker Landing (old-timers called it Graddock Landing) on the west side of the Intracoastal Waterway (then Pablo Creek); mainly pine trees and a few small cypress are present. Intracoastal boats are transporting goods through the shallow waters between what is now Palm Valley and Nocatee, circa 1916. *From the Beaches Area Historical Society Collection.*

There are bits of "Old Dixie Highway" in the Durbin, Florida and Hilden, Florida areas, but modern construction has separated them from the main U.S. Highway 1 line.

U.S. Highway 1

The eastern portion of the Dixie Highway running south from Jacksonville, Florida, and including Bayard to St. Augustine, was largely replaced with U.S. Highway 1.

U.S. 1 largely follows the route of the Atlantic Highway and originally shared the same termini of Fort Kent, Maine, and Miami, Florida. The section from Miami, Florida, to Jacksonville, Florida, duplicates the Dixie Highway. The names of the old auto trails are still used locally in many places.[116]

The U.S. numbered highway system is the oldest remaining numbering system in Florida. Florida first assigned numbers to its state roads in about 1917, but posting may not have occurred until 1923. In 1946, the old Florida road numbering system was done away with in favor of the current grid system. There are a few vestiges of the old state road numbering system left in the Sunshine State. The traveler interested in historical routes will find it easier to

Oblique view of the south side of the western end of the drawbridge, the operator's house and the southwest fender, facing northeast. Palm Valley Bridge, County Road 210, spanned the Intracoastal Waterway and Ponte Vedra Beach, St. Johns County. Mickler Palm Valley Bridge (1900s) was the third bridge built over the Intracoastal Waterway. The new overhead bridge has replaced this drawbridge, now extending into Nocatee. *Library of Congress Prints and Photographs Division, Washington, D.C.*

follow older alignments of the U.S. highway system, which has been in use in Florida since 1926.[117]

U.S. 1 has been around since the earliest planning stages; it is in the 1925 Bureau of Public Roads (BPR) plan, for example. In 1927, it entered the state south of Folkston, Georgia. It was routed through Jacksonville, Durbin, St. Augustine, Daytona, Titusville, Melbourne, Fort Pierce and West Palm Beach and ended in Miami at Florida City. The original route largely followed the east or "main" leg of the Dixie Highway. Heading south, U.S. 1 followed a route close to its current alignment. In Jacksonville, Old King's Road is the original U.S. 1. The route was moved back east from Goodbys over Old St. Augustine Road to join with the current alignment at Bayard. By 1935, U.S. 1 had become a straight shot between south Jacksonville and Bayard. U.S. 1 then ran south through Durbin (Ponte Vedra) on its way to St. Augustine.[118]

JACKSONVILLE, ST. AUGUSTINE & HALIFAX RIVER RAILWAY (1883); JACKSONVILLE, ST. AUGUSTINE & INDIAN RIVER RAILWAY (1892); AND FLORIDA EAST COAST RAILWAY (1895)

The first railroad tracks actually built in Diego Plains (Palm Valley, now Ponte Vedra) were adjacent to Old Dixie Highway on the west side of Diego Plains. They were built from Jacksonville to St. Augustine and were completed in 1883. This first railroad was the Jacksonville, St. Augustine & Halifax Railway (JStA&HR), a narrow-gauge railroad that was opened for business on June 28, 1883.

By October 29, 1883, there were seven stations between St. Augustine and Jacksonville on Old Dixie Highway. The station adjacent to the Palm Valley area was then called Durbin, located at Diego about halfway between the two cities of Jacksonville and St. Augustine.

The JStA&HR Railway was purchased by Henry Flagler on December 31, 1885. In 1892, the railway was renamed the Jacksonville, St. Augustine & Indian River Railway (JStA&IR).

On September 7, 1895, the name was changed again, to the Florida East Coast Railway (FEC); that railway operates through the Palm Valley area, which today is adjacent to and on the west side of Philips Highway/Route 1. At that time, the FEC was the only means of public transportation from Palm Valley or Diego Plains for residents traveling to Jacksonville or St. Augustine.

In 1895, the FEC only traveled to the south side of Jacksonville's St. Johns River. There was no bridge built across the St. Johns River until much later to connect to the other northbound railroads.

Second Spanish Period in North Florida

1783–1821

Spanish Regain Control

The Second Spanish Period lasted for thirty-eight years, from 1783 to 1821. Spanish forces marched into west Florida in 1779, during the Revolutionary War (1775–83). Under the Treaty of Paris in 1783, after twenty years of British rule, St. Augustine and Florida were returned to Spain. By the time the Spanish reclaimed Florida, their world power had weakened considerably. Spain was faced with the dilemma of having too few colonists, forcing it to give up its policy of requiring settlers to convert to Catholicism. This encouraged many English planters to return to Florida in the early 1800s. Generous grants were awarded to well-placed whites willing to develop northeast Florida lands into productive plantations.

Spain found little but trouble during its second tenure of Florida. Spanish colonists, as well as settlers from the newly formed United States, came pouring in when the British evacuated Florida. Many of the new residents were lured by favorable Spanish terms for acquiring property, called land grants. Others were escaped slaves, trying to reach a place where their U.S. masters had no authority and effectively could not reach them. In 1812, a group of eastern Florida settlers rebelled and declared their independence from Spain. But the Spaniards stopped the rebels. Instead of becoming more Spanish, Florida increasingly became more "American."[119]

As a growing white population in the American South forced settlers to develop less fertile lands nearer Indian territories, the settlers looked hungrily across the St. Mary's River at the abundance of fertile land in Spanish

In 1783, a new Spanish flag was designed, and it stood until 1821, when Spain transferred all of Florida to the United States after the Second Spanish Period ended. *National Park Service, U.S. Department of the Interior.*

Florida. To incorporate these eager settlers, Spain in 1790 decreed a homesteading land grant policy with acreage based on head rights: one hundred acres to the head of the household and fifty acres to other members of the household, including slaves.

After ten years of cultivation and construction of prescribed buildings, the settlers could receive clear title to the land Mediterranean settlers introduced into Florida as laborers in 1768 during the British period; these settlers remained when the Spanish returned in 1784. The majority, from the Mediterranean island of Minorca, became known as "Minorcans."

In 1777, they abandoned the New Smyrna plantation, relocated to St. Augustine and took advantage of the headrights decree. Both banks of the North River were favored locations for Minorcan grants because of those people's familiarity with the practice of rice cultivation in marsh settings. The mainland riverfront and the Guana Peninsula became home to a concentration of Minorcan settlements.[120]

THE MINORCAN RESIDENTS

When the British evacuation began in 1783, the Minorcans were in opportune positions to acquire farmlands at minimal prices. Juan and Thomas Andreu were the first to began cultivating small tracts at Grant's Villa. The Spanish census of 1786 lists Juan Andreu on the six acres he previously rented from David Yeats. A water well lined with coquina stone constructed during Andreu's time still stands on the shell bank (at Guana).

So many Minorcan families established settlements along the North and Guana Rivers that a special section of the 1797 Spanish census was dubbed the "North River Settlements." In 1804, Andreu received royal title to 160 acres that he named "White Oyster Shell Bank Plantation."

Just south of this was a 367-acre piece owned by Jose Peso de Burgo, a native of Corsica who moved to this tract in 1786, calling the northern section San Genaro and the southern part El Burgos. Like most of the Minorcans of St. Augustine, De Burgo; his wife, Maria Mabrity de Burgo; and a daughter lived in the Minorcan quarter of town (St. Augustine) and traveled by day to the farm at North River or the estate on the San Sebastian River. By the time De Burgo died in 1818, he had become a merchant, the owner of substantial rural acreage and the owner of twelve slaves.

De Burgo's widow, Maria Mabrity, married a second time, to Juan Andreu II, and they combined the acreage they each had inherited to create the most significant landholding on the former site of Grant's Villa.

Antonio Andreu, another brother of Juan Andreu's, purchased a homestead at the former site of Grant's Villa from Lorenzo Capella in 1804, known as Santa Catalina Plantation. Miguel and Jose, sons of Antonio, received a 103-acre service grant, the "Chimneys" of Governor Grant, for their military contributions. In 1829, Miguel Andreu purchased San Ignacio from Juan Segui, originally granted to Lazaro Ortega. San Ignacio stayed in Miguel Andreu's hands for only three years and was sold to Ramon Sabate on February 17, 1832, with Sabate retaining ownership throughout the remainder of the century.

The land south of the "Chimneys" where Grant's overseers had resided, was also divided into small tracts and granted to Minorcan settlers. Mariano Fontan, Antonio Caballero and Jose Hernandez Carmona claimed ownership of the tract immediately south of the "Chimneys" and fought one another in court for years to gain clear title. Eventually, part of a one-hundred-acre tract was awarded to Fontan.[121]

James R. Hanham, a former captain in the United States Army, was one of the few non-Minorcans who bought property in the area. Soon after the purchase, however, Hanham experienced economic hardship and let the land lay fallow until Charles Seton acquired it in May 1826. Phillip R. Yong bought the tract in 1832. Following Yong's death in 1853, this property, El Burgo, was retained by successive generations of the Yong family until the 1920s.

DIEGO PLAINS PROPERTY OWNERS—SPANISH LAND GRANTS, 1797–1836

Events north of the border (in Georgia) kept Spanish east Florida in a state of tension. Georgians made an unsuccessful invasion in 1795. Although Florida remained Spanish in spite of the invasion, settlers had been uprooted and suffered destruction. Some of them abandoned the province.[122]

Runaway slaves ("contraband") also sought freedom in the Spanish colony. Many U.S. citizens considered Florida a sanctuary for their nation's enemies. Land-hungry settlers also considered Florida an easy target for territorial expansion. These factors eventually led to the notorious 1818 invasion of

Spanish Florida by Andrew Jackson, during which he executed two British citizens for treason. Jackson's battles with Florida's Indian people would later be called the First Seminole War in 1835. President James Monroe later appointed General Andrew Jackson to be the first governor of Florida.

Finally, after several official and unofficial U.S. military expeditions into the territory, Spain formally ceded Florida to the United States in 1821, according to terms of the Adams-Onis Treaty.

Following are a few examples of the will transfers of north Florida residents back in the 1800s.

- The will, in 1797, of Josefa de la Encarnacion Espinosa, legitimate daughter of Diego Espinosa and Josefa Torres, named her nephew, Jose Sanchez, and Francisco Xavier Miranda as administrators of her estate.

- The heirs of Sebastian Espinosa were granted by Governor White five hundred acres in Diego Plains at Wueridge (Uleridge), north of Francisco Xavier Sanchez's land. Espinosa had held them until his death in 1819.

- Francisco Xavier Sanchez and heirs were granted 255 acres from a plantation named Sabana General. Mary Dewees inherited them, and the daughter of Francisco Xavier Sanchez sold them to Thomas Fitch.

- The heirs of Thomas Fitch were granted four hundred acres (sold by Francisco Roman Sanchez, heirs of Francisco Xavier Sanchez) on Plains of Diego, Llano de San Diego.

- Juan Gonzales was granted one thousand acres, called "Levet," in San Diego Plains.

- Espinosa was granted five hundred acres at Wellridge, San Diego Plains, by Governor Coppinger.

- Christina Hill Sanchez, widow of Joseph Sanchez, was granted 405 acres (50 acres in Casino Loco and the rest in Diego Plains).

- Christina Hill and others—heirs of Pedro Miranda and heirs of Maria Andre Sanchez, all heirs of the late Josefe Espinosa and Sebastian, her brother—sold to Luis Mattain four caballeries and 7 acres, 150 acres total, at San Ramon for 150 pesos cash.

- Andres Papy claimed 126 acres at Fort San Diego. Philip Solano bought them from the heirs of Espinosa and sold to Anna Pons, February 9, 1819. Felipe Solana sold to Ana Pons, a widow, three caballerias[123] and 26 acres at the plantation called Fort of San Diego for $126 on February 1, 1819.

- Andres Burgevin was granted the plot west of San Diego Swamp, called "San Ramo," in 1820.

- A plat of 190.91 acres at San Ramon was granted to Luis Mattain in 1836.[124]

Throughout the period, United States sentiment for the annexation of Florida increased. A period of crisis was reached in 1812, when the United States attempted to invade and occupy Florida. The effects of this movement had a major impact on the residents of St. Johns County, many of whom had their farms and plantations burned during these incursions.[125]

For thirty-eight years during this Second Spanish Period, the area that was to become Palm Valley and Ponte Vedra consisted of several large Spanish land grants. The occupants of these grants built haciendas and tried to establish Spanish culture, but frequent raids by Native Americans made life here far less than tranquil. Long after Florida became a state (in 1845), rattlesnakes, alligators and billions of mosquitoes occupied the current location of Palm Valley/Ponte Vedra.

The largest Spanish land grants shown on the 1834 map by Deputy Surveyor Henry Washington were owned by the following:

- Pedro Mestre, 640 acres granted in 1825
- Ben Chairs/Chaires, 80 acres granted in 1828
- Pedro Miranda, 1,000 acres granted in 1824
- Pedro R. de Calla heirs, 200 acres granted in 1825
- Davis Floyd, 832.93 acres granted in 1825
- Nicholas Sanchez heirs, 300 acres granted, called "Quiqui"
- Mosés E. Levy, 276 acres granted
- Davis Jones, 10 acres granted in 1825
- Thomas Fitch, 255 acres granted
- Thomas Fitch heirs, 171 and 302.77 acres (separate) granted
- Francis X. Sanchez, 96 acres and 100 acres (separate) granted
- Pedro Cocifacio, 500 acres granted
- Andres Papy, 127.83 acres granted
- Sebastian Espinosa, 333 acres granted
- Joseph S. Sanchez, 608.47 acres granted[126]

Reenactment of Spanish soldiers landing on the Ponte Vedra shoreline in the sixteenth century, from *Conquest of America* (History Channel). *From the* Jacksonville (FL) Times-Union.

St. Johns County is significant in the area of exploration/settlement. It has been occupied continuously since 1565, making it the oldest settled county in the United States. St. Johns contains more Spanish land grants than any other county in the state.[127]

Nicholas Sanchez (and his heirs) was apparently the owner of three hundred acres on Diego Plains at a place called "Quiqui," which was penciled in on the 1834 survey map at the St. Augustine Historical Society in a location adjacent to the northeast corner of the Pedro Mestre property. The only other mention of "Quiqui" that was noted referred to the years "before 1819," when the land was cultivated and improved with fences, houses and other buildings.[128]

Solana (mistaken for "Solano") Road is later also erroneously named after the Spanish military leader Felipe Solana Sr., who negotiated with the victorious British. The road was actually named after Manuel Lorenzo Solana, one of the "Mounted Dragoons" of the Spanish army in St. Augustine who survived through the First Spanish, British and Second Spanish Periods.

During this time, the United States was anxious to acquire both east and west Florida. The vast, largely undeveloped area was a temptation for the expansionist government and for private land speculators. East Florida in particular provided a setting for contraband trade and slave smuggling, both of which were in conflict with the policies and laws of the United States government during the period. Finally, because of their strategic importance, east and west Florida potentially threatened the national security of the United States. They could potentially serve as bases for attacking the United States if acquired by a foreign power.[129]

Throughout this period, United States sentiment for the annexation of Florida increased. A period of crisis was reached in 1812, when the United States attempted to invade and occupy Florida.[130] The effects of this movement had a major impact on the residents of St. Johns County, many of whom had their farms and plantations burned during these incursions. The destructive activities and the ensuing occupation of Florida by hostile troops prevented many of the residents of the countryside from using their lands and labor forces and severely stymied the economic development of Florida. Many rural residents left Spanish Florida in frustration.[131]

The United States government wanted to annex Florida to prevent its use by foreign powers and to control the activities of runaway slaves and relocated Native Americans.[132] The United States did not actually pay any money to Spain for Florida. However, the government agreed to pay $5 million from U.S. citizens for property damages. Finally, after several official and unofficial U.S. military expeditions into the territory, Spain formally ceded Florida to the United States in 1821, according to terms of the Adams-Onis Treaty.[133]

Andrew Jackson returned to Florida in 1821 to establish a new territorial government on behalf of the United States. What the U.S. government inherited was a wilderness sparsely dotted with settlements of native Indian people, African Americans and Spaniards. In a very short time, these new settlers wished to join the Union, but at first they could not agree as to whether Florida should be made into one or two states. Finally, however, it was decided that it should be one, and in March 1845, it was admitted to the Union as a slave state.[134]

Most histories of the Second Spanish Period of east Florida, which retained the same borders as the British colony of that name, reflect the Anglophilic viewpoints of earlier historians—that is, viewpoints admiring of British customs/culture. The era is generally portrayed as an interval of decline wedged between the British and American periods, merely awaiting an inevitable takeover by the United States and its institutions. That view arose largely from reliance on English-language sources, which aggrandized conditions during those two periods while minimizing developments during the Spanish Period.[135]

PONTEVEDRA, SPAIN, AND PONTE VEDRA BEACH, FLORIDA

800,000 BC to present

LOCATION IN IBERIA

The first indication of human habitation in Spain was on the Iberian Peninsula (where Spain is located), which dates from approximately 800,000 BC. The Iberian peninsula, or Iberia, is located in the extreme southwest of Europe. It is bordered on the south and east by the Mediterranean Sea and on the north and west by the Atlantic Ocean. The Pyrenees form the northeast edge of the peninsula, connecting it to the rest of Europe. At Gibraltar in the south, it approaches Africa.[136]

In medieval times, the peninsula housed many small countries. However, these amalgamated over time until the end of the Napoleonic Wars (including the peninsula) in 1815. At that point, the modern configuration was reached, and the peninsula now consists of the countries of Spain and Portugal (excluding their islands and Ceuta and Melilla), as well as Andorra and the territory of Gibraltar.

The province of Pontevedra, Spain, on the Iberian Peninsula lies in the far southwest of Galicia. To the north is the province of Coruna, and to the east are Lugo and Orense. In the south, the River Miño lies between Pontevedra and Portugal, whereas in the west we find the well-known Rías Baixas, with their popular beaches that border the Atlantic Ocean. The entire province covers an area of more than 4,400 square kilometers and is the smallest of the four Galician provinces. Nevertheless, it is the province with the most varied scenery of all and with the highest density of population (204 inhabitants per square kilometer in 1988), most of whom are located in the areas nearest the sea.

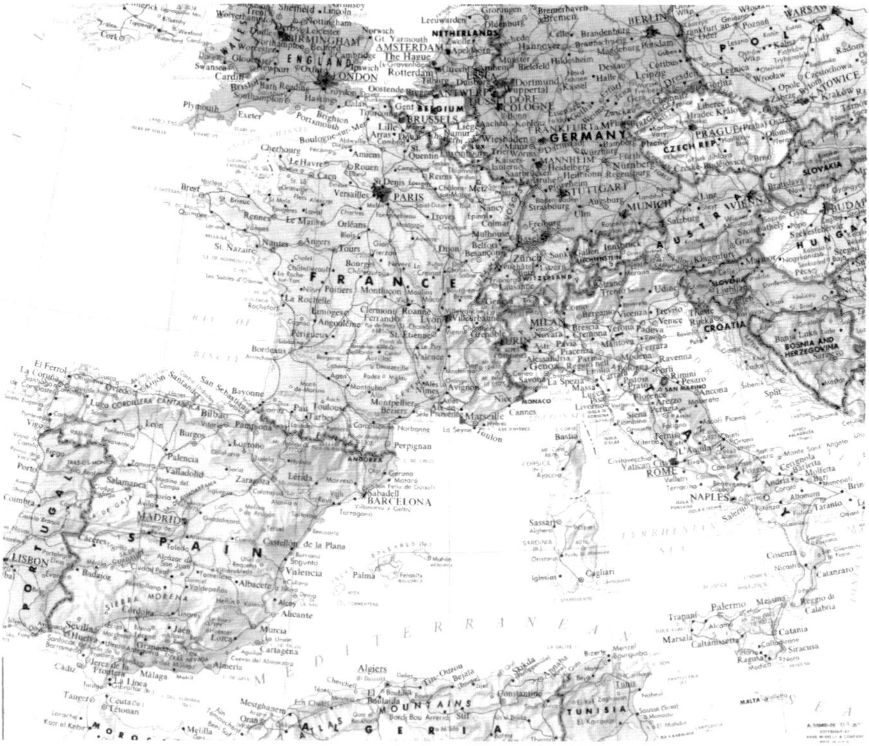

Map of Pontevedra, Spain, which is our sister city and the place from which our name was derived. It is one of the few Spanish cities on the Atlantic coast of Spain, which has a far different heritage and background than our Florida city. *Rand McNally & Company, copyright A-558300-26,* Mediterranean Lands.

Pontevedra Meaning

The city's name is said to derive from "Pontem Veteram/Pontis Veteris" (Old Bridge) but could equally as well come from "Ponte de Piedra" (Bridge of Stone). The earliest records of its existence as a focus for commercial activities go back to the twelfth century.

Pontevedra, "Boa Vila" ("Good Town") was the title of a book published in 1947, and that title, which echoes a popular saying, undoubtedly sums up the whole philosophy of "the city of the camellia." This is a town with a high quality of life, a positive civic value, a tranquility in its streets and a benevolence in its countryside. Its historical center is, as all scholars recognize, one of the richest in the region, second only to Santiago de Compostela.

Pictures of Spain's Pontevedra all feature an "old bridge" in the foreground. The town has a Gothic church and a fine Roman bridge—the "Pons Vetus" from which the city derives its name, meaning "Old Bridge" in Latin.[137]

THE TOWN'S ATTRACTIONS

Three squares make up the most distinctive parts of the historic town. First is the Praza de Ferrería, the traditional center, with its great sixteenth-century fountain and the San Francisco Monastery. Second is the Praza de Teucro, named after the legendary founder of this capital of the Rías Baixas ("Low Estuaries"); the eighteenth-century palaces are particularly remarkable here. And finally is the typical and secluded Praza de A Leña, with its nostalgic significance for all the people of Pontevedra.

Whenever someone wishes to contemplate a real artistic anthology in a small space, they have it nearby in the rupestrian engravings in the surrounding area; the great collection of prehistoric goldsmith and jet-stone artifacts in the Provincial Museum; the emblazoned façades; the magnificent masonry of the monasteries of Lerez and Poio; the Romanesque style present in San Mamed de Moldes; the Baroque style present in the San Bartolomé Church; the monastery of Sant Clara y La Peregrina (symbol of Pontevedra, with its floor plan in the shape of a scallop shell); the Gothic style present in the ruins of Santo Domindo and the gallery of the castle of Stotomayor, twelve kilometres away; the Ogival style present in San Francisco; or Isabelline and Plateresque in Santa María la Mayor.

Whenever someone wishes to follow tourist routes from Pontevedra, he has a more difficult choice. One may look inland, heading for Ourense or Santiago, and the triangle of Caldas de Reis, La Hermida and Ponte Caldelas offers all the suggestiveness of Galicia. If one seeks the sea, one only has to look to the estuary, and in the background the island of Tambo can be seen, as was sung by Góngora. In the foreground is the mouth of the River Lérez, and on all sides are some of the best beaches to be found in Galicia; the marvel of the *cruceiro* (stone cross) at San Andrés de Hío, representing the descent of Christ; the wealth of *hórreos* (raised granaries) in Combarro, houses with complex family crests; the vineyards of Albariño; the lands of Salnés, where Ramón del Valle-Inclán was inspired; the grandeur of La Lanzada; the serenity of all the land of Arousa; the eternal homage to shellfish in "O Grove"; and the charm of A Toxa (La Toja).

Today, Pontevedra is not just a "boa vila." It is "boa terra" (good land), "boa mar" (good sea) and "boa la cocina" (good cooking), which is, of course, enviable. There are those who say that, all together, it is one of the last paradises. Many believe this to be true. Galicia, Spain's westernmost province, is blessed with moderate weather, adorned with beautiful beaches and inculcated with Spanish and Celtic roots. This mélange has given rise to a true Gallegan spirit, a culture within a larger Spanish culture—one with its own customs and even language but also one that is quintessimally the characteristics that we search out—a bit off the beaten path. Open, friendly, jovial, vibrant…all define the

Galician natives. These are the characteristics that we search out—a heritage that goes back to Helen of Troy.

History and folklore tell of a Trojan archer named Teucer, son of Telemon, half-brother of Ajax, who, following the Trojan War, journeyed to what would become Spain and founded Pontevedra. It originally had a Trojan name but was later (and historians say originally) named by the Romans Pons Vetus. Pontevedra is also one of four cities to claim Christopher Columbus as its native son that we know to be incorrect. The Columbus myth almost certainly arises from the belief that one of his ships, the *Santa Maria*, was built in the town's yards and launched there as *La Gallega*. However, this is quite likely to be a myth as well. Its other (and true) famous son was the father of Fidel Castro, who migrated from Galicia to Cuba, where he became a successful sugar cane plantation owner.

Pontevedra's patron saint is San Sebastian, but the town's real patron is the Virgin Mary, more specifically La Virgan de la O. More often, she is referred to as the Virxen Peregrina. You can translate this as either the Virgin of Pilgrimage or as the Wandering Virgin. Statues of her adorn the town, and larger versions are carried in the several religious processions that take place during the year.

Pontevedra is built on and of granite, or at least the older buildings are, as are most of the houses in the hills. This makes for a truly imposing old quarter in the town itself, but it has been said that the countryside is very much a mixed bag. There are some outstandingly beautiful houses built with weathered, high-quality granite, but there are also many garish monstrosities built in new, lighter, cheaper granite.

MAKEUP OF PONTEVEDRA'S PROVINCE

The four capitals shown on the map near the beginning of the chapter, consisting of Lugo, Orense, La Coruna and Pontevedra, make up the province of Galicia, Spain. The Galicia Province is the only one in Spain that borders on the Atlantic coast. As you can note, Pontevedra is the only capital area of Galicia to border on both the Atlantic Ocean and Portugal areas.

The names of the areas that make up the province of Pontevedra in Spain's Galicia Providence include Argolada, A Caniza, A Estrada, A Guarda, A Lama, Arbo, As Neves, Baiona, Barro, Bueu, Caldas, Cambadox, Campo Lameiro, Cangas, Catoira, Cerdedo, Cotobade, Covele, Crecente, Cuntis, Dozon, Forcarey, Fornelos, Gondamar, Lalin, Marin, Meano, Meis, Moana, Mondariz, Mondariz Balneario, Morana, Mos, Nigran, O Crove, O Rosal, Oia, Poio, Ponteareas, Pontecaldelas, Pontecesures, Pontevedra, Porrino, Portas, Redondela, Ribadumia, Rodeiro, Salceda, Salvatierra, Sanxenxo, Silleda, Soutomaior, Tomino, Tui, Valga, Vigo, Vila de Cruc, Vilaboa, Vilagarcia and Vilanova.

THE PONTEVEDRA–PONTE VEDRA BEACH CONNECTION

In 1995, Ponte Vedra Beach residents Jack Morgan and Bill Hill decided over dinner one night that it would be quite natural to form a sister city relationship between Pontevedra and its American namesake.[138] "My enthusiasm for this has been to create a Ponte Vedra Beach community project to give people a sense of identity with their town," said Morgan. That conversation between two friends grew into Friends Across the Sea (between Ponte Vedra Beach and Pontevedra, Spain).

The Rotary Club of Ponte Vedra Beach joined with Friends Across the Sea to organize a pen pal program with local schools and some student exchanges. In 1977, Friends hosted twenty-four Pontevedrans, who visited Ponte Vedra Beach, St. Augustine and Jacksonville. The 2002 return to Ponte Vedra Beach was the culmination of several years of efforts to create a cultural and economic exchange. This exchange, while educational at the time, was not to last, and the visits began to diminish.

Although they share similar names, are linked by a Spanish heritage and face each other across the Atlantic Ocean, there is a world of difference between

The Intracoastal boat ramp is as new as the new bridge over the waterway and is a much-improved and accessible ramp for small boats to enjoy the canal. *Photo by M. Robinson, 2008.*

The seventeenth hole of the Players Championship is played in golf's most prestigious tournament, with the TPC held each year at Sawgrass, headquarters for the PGA. *From a Players Championship publication, 2006, Ponte Vedra Beach, Florida.*

the two Ponte Vedras. Ponte Vedra Beach is a seaside mecca of golf, tennis and beautiful beaches; Pontevedra, Spain, sits not on the ocean but rather near the coast, at the head of a fjord-like river running to the sea.

As Ponte Vedra Beach can trace its Spanish roots back to 1513, Pontevedra, Spain, is a medieval town that attributes its origins to a Greek sailor and Trojan War hero, dating back to the twelfth century.

The Stockton Connection in North Florida

1920s

There are only a handful of individuals whose energy and ambition helped shape the course and direction of Jacksonville and Ponte Vedra's history in the late nineteenth and early twentieth centuries.[139] Few of these individuals contributed more to the city and Ponte Vedra's successful growth than Telfair Stockton, patriarch of a family whose name is synonymous with northeast Florida and Ponte Vedra. Telfair began his real estate venture in 1884, and in 1902, the company name was Stockton & Budd.

From 1884 to 2006, the Stockton family was destined to maintain a close involvement with the city of Jacksonville and Ponte Vedra communities. Telfair Stockton, son James R. Stockton and grandson James Jr. have left undeniable marks on the area.

If Julia Stockton had not moved to Jacksonville after the Civil War, and if her son, Telfair, had not proved to possess the business acumen he had, this area would not be what it is. "Ju" Stockton opened a boardinghouse in 1870 after the death of her husband, Will. "She had seven mouths to feed. Then Grandfather, in 1884, started Telfair Stockton & Company," reported Jim Stockton Jr. The rest, so to speak, is history.

From a newsstand set up when he was sixteen to the organization of the Florida Printing and Publishing Company, Telfair Stockton and his brothers bought control of every major new daily in Jacksonville, including the *Florida Times-Union* in 1888. Real estate soon became his first love, and by 1893, when the first James Roosevelt Stockton was born, Telfair Stockton & Company was well established as a leading development firm. (The Roosevelt connection enters through Julia Fitch, Telfair Stockton's wife, who was a relative of President Theodore Roosevelt.)

In the years following Jacksonville's "Great Fire of 1901," Telfair Stockton began specializing in residential construction and later shifted the focus to the creation of entire communities. Telfair was an innovator in employing the first large-scale use of newspaper advertising in promoting their residential communities. The Telfair Stockton & Company real estate firm was officially established in 1910. Joined by his son, James R. Stockton Sr., Telfair began drawing plans for his first large-scale residential developments in the early 1920s. Thus did the subdivisions of Avondale and San Marco on each side of the St. Johns River come about. In the late 1920s, a string of other successful developments followed, including the first major effort at large-scale real estate development in Ponte Vedra.

Telfair was a member of the state legislature in 1923, but upon Telfair's death in 1932, James continued to build on his father's legacy and, in 1946, founded Stockton, Whatley, Davin & Company (SWD). Soon, SWD became one of Florida's largest real estate firms.

The National Lead Company (NLC) brought in Telfair Stockton & Company in 1937 to manage the Ponte Vedra Properties, and in 1942, that company purchased the properties from National Lead. During this time, a 110-unit inn was constructed, along with the patio and cottage units. The Innlet was constructed 1939 with 32 rooms and 20 apartments.

Live oak tree with hanging Spanish moss on the property of Jimmie Stockton. *Photo by Ellen Diamond, 2012.*

JAMES STOCKTON'S PURCHASE

Jimmy's father, James, drove the first large-scale development in Ponte Vedra Beach. "First of all, this was a long way from nowhere back then," Jimmy Stockton said. "And World War II was underway. Nobody knew then how things were going to turn out. National Lead came to my dad and asked him to sell their Ponte Vedra property. He told them that nobody would buy it. So they came back and asked my dad if he'd be interested."

NLC wanted $2 million and was even willing to carry a note for the entire amount. Stockton, however, would go no higher than $500,000. NLC subsequently accepted the deal, and Telfair Stockton & Company assumed control of the inland property, the oceanfront, the club and the golf course, which had been expanded to eighteen holes. "Dad was a great visionary," Jimmy Stockton recalled.[140]

In 1942, the senior Stockton bought the club property for $500,000. Three years later, he paid the same sum of $500,000 for ten thousand acres, including five miles of oceanfront land in what is now known as the Guana Reserve. Telfair Stockton & Company merged with Whatley, Davin & Company in 1947.[141]

Included in the purchase from National Lead were more than six miles of oceanfront at South Ponte Vedra Beach. James Stockton Sr., then president of the company, directed the further improvements on the land, placing particular emphasis on its ecological conservation. A dam was built in 1958 on the Guana River that then formed the 2,200-acre Guana Lake, now one of the finest fishing spots and wildlife preserves in this part of Florida.[142]

In 1959, the third generation of the Stockton family entered the family real estate business. James R. Stockton's son (and the grandson of Telfair Stockton), James "Jimmy" R. Stockton Jr., joined in the family real estate business until later venturing out on his own. Jimmy Stockton grew up with his family at 419 Ponte Vedra Boulevard on the beach just south of the Ponte Vedra Inn & Club. However, after he married Victoria, he moved with his family a little farther down the beach to the 1300 block.

Upon James R. Stockton Jr.'s graduation from Washington and Lee University in Virginia, he served on active duty in the United States Marine Corps. He began his working career in 1959 at Stockton, Whatley, Davin & Company and left in 1966 to form his own company. Jimmy Stockton had a dream to follow in his dad's footsteps, and Jimmy is basically responsible for Sawgrass. He's the reason it's here today. It was the first project of such a magnitude in which there were no environmental complaints at all! And this was during the '70s, when there was so much consciousness about the environment. James Stockton Jr. was one of the finer developers and a very compassionate person.[143]

The Ponte Vedra Inn & Club, with its alligator fountain, is reminiscent of the time when alligators roamed throughout the Ponte Vedra Beach area, then called Mineral City. *From* Legacy, *a magazine of the Ponte Vedra Inn & Club, 2003.*

In 1966, James formed his own company, Stockton Land Corporation, with the goal of concentrating on the creation of new residential communities in Ponte Vedra Beach and other major projects, including his development of Ponte Vedra's most definitive landmark: the Sawgrass Country Club.[144]

In the late 1960s, Ponte Vedra Beach was isolated, as there was no easy access to Jacksonville. In 1970, when Jimmy Stockton was in Africa on safari, he got the idea to develope the Sawgrass Country Club and Resort (like his father did for the Ponte Vedra Inn & Club). He started purchasing land when he returned from Africa. He first purchased six hundred acres west of the boulevard and later purchased five hundred acres on the oceanfront from the Land Corporation of America for $100,000.

In July 1971, Jimmy Stockton Jr. presented plans for developing 200 acres, two miles below the Innlet, and was approved by the Community Association Board with a three-story limit east and four-story limit west of Ponte Vedra Boulevard. In 1972, he began the challenging development of the now famous Sawgrass Country Club. The groundbreaking for this 1,100-acre development of Sawgrass was held that year. In 1975, Stockton Land Corporation–Realtors became a major force in the "First Coast" real estate market.

Tourist/guests fishing in a boat at the Ponte Vedra Inn & Club's lake, 1948. *Florida Memory, Division of Library & Information Services, Tallahassee, Florida.*

The sawgrass growing on the dunes at the beach offer shoreline beauty and protection for the ocean waves coming ashore. *Photo by Ellen Diamond, 2012.*

In the early '70s, Jimmy Stockton Jr. and his family purchased more than 1,600 feet of oceanfront land and more than five hundred acres of undeveloped land from Frank Kelly, a developer from Chicago who had seen the potential of this area early on. This purchase was to become Sawgrass. They wanted a development that would be environmentally acceptable—a blend of town homes, condos, conventional homes, golf courses and lakes. The idea worked, as well over one hundred units were sold the first year.

THE SAWGRASS NAME

Jimmy Stockton had a very difficult time coming up with a name for this new development. After many different choices were offered, Stockton thought that there were as many suggested names as there was sawgrass in the area. The final choice of name was inspired by these widespread, beautiful local plants.

But why "Sawgrass?" How did the name evolve? "It almost didn't," Jim Stockton said as he chuckled behind his full red beard, acquired since his early Sawgrass days.

> *We knew we had to have a name for legal requirements. But nothing stuck. Our creative team, the core of our very existence as a land company, was made up of Ed Seay* [golf architect]*, Don Cheek* [land planner] *and Al Hammack* [chief engineer]. *We batted the idea around for weeks, trying out every name we could think of and some we shouldn't have. Clichés, most of them, like Sea Spray, Ocean Wilds, Dune Village, junk like that. Then, as I was trying to go to sleep one night, churning and tossing over a tangle of names, I almost gave up. It's growing wild, I said to myself, like all that sawgrass on the property.*

The co-founder and editor of the *Ponte Vedra Recorder* wrote in one of her early columns that Jim Stockton dropped into her office on October 12, 1972, and brought with him the master plan for his new real estate venture south of Ponte Vedra. She wrote, "It would be called 'Sawgrass,' he said, because there was so much of it on the property."[145]

The scope of the project consisted of about 1,100 acres encompassing single-family lots, residential homes and condominiums on the oceanfront, as well as around the lakes and golf courses. Stockton was the first to move into a condo in Sawgrass Country Club in February 1974, the year that 140 properties were sold.[146] The whole theme of the project was one of "elegant informality," with emphasis on the ecological preservation of the basic land, Stockton added. According to him, there will be initiation fees, and people may

Storm fence along the beaches dunes, with sawgrass growing for protection from the storms that wash away the sand. *Photo by Ellen Diamond, 2012.*

Sawgrass Village opening on March 17, 1984, where $500 was presented to BAHS by Bill Shuben, president of Arvida Commercial and Industrial Division. Mrs. Jean McCormick (Mrs. J.T.), president of BAHS, accepts the check. *From the Beaches Area Historical Society Collection.*

be members of the various clubs without actually being property owners. His plans do not include a hotel, and all members will eventually be property owners of the development.[147] However, it trailed off drastically, as Ponte Vedra was still somewhat isolated. J. Turner Butler Boulevard was not complete, and the oil embargo in 1974 kept people from traveling.

In 1974, the development of Sawgrass opened for golf. However, the development (like many others in the country) was slashed by the high interest rates (greater than 15 percent) and inflation. James Stockton Jr. deeded Sawgrass to a consortium of banks to keep the development afloat. During this period, there were only about 450 homes in Ponte Vedra Beach.

In 1977, the Arvida Corporation, which was founded by Arthur Vining Davis in 1956 and which acquired Penn Central in the 1960s, a subsidiary of Penn Central Corporation, purchased the Sawgrass property. It had a track record with resort and residential property in other Florida areas. With an improving economy, plenty of gas and the completion of J. Turner Butler Boulevard, sales once again began to pick up. In 1984, Walt Disney Productions acquired Arvida.

The overall Sawgrass record after ten years in the making was first under James Stockton's creative yet economically plagued leadership, then under Arvida's determined administration. Sawgrass Village was the capstone of the vivid reminder of James Stockton's original vision. In October 1971, when

Aerial view of the Ponte Vedra Inn & Club in 1928, as well as 2003 at the Ocean Course, golf hole no. 9. *From* Legacy, *a magazine of the Ponte Vedra Inn & Club, 2003.*

announcing plans for his still unnamed community, he said it would "include condominiums, private residences, a golf course, a bath club and a shopping complex." All have now come to pass, even though it took ten years and implementation by another company for the final peg to fall in place.[148]

The entire Stockton family, including Telfair, James R. and James Jr., have been intimately involved in the development of what was initially called Mineral City (from 1914 to 1928, now Ponte Vedra), as well as Jacksonville. Their foresight and initiative have been some of the key steppingstones for the residential development of both areas.

In April 2005, Jimmy Stockton found himself in a conversation with Herb Peyton, discussing the possibility of joining a national resort real estate consortium. "Herb wasn't interested," Stockton noted, "but he said, 'Let's talk.'" After this exchange, Peyton's Ponte Vedra Club Realty purchased Stockton Realty and the building occupied by Stockton's property management offices, although it kept the Stockton name.[149]

THE FIRST PONTE VEDRA NEWSPAPERS

1963 to present

PONTE VEDRA RECORDER, VOLUME NO. 1, NOVEMBER 7, 1969

Peg Bradford and Gretchen Carpenter established the one-page monthly *Recorder* to provide a link between members of the growing community. Tim Bradford took over from his mother and established a sixteen-page weekly that kept everyone updated on our community's news and had a positive impact on the county's quality of life.

In the 1990s, the *Recorder* developed a new section, "Bridges," that focuses on the softer side of the news and on citizens whose souls shape the community. Dedication to the community goes beyond reporting the daily events that shape the lives of its residents. It means providing extras that give readers an edge.

In 1999, after thirty years of family ownership, the *Recorder* was sold to Add Inc., with headquarters in Wisconsin. Today, the weekly publication of the *Recorder*, more than ever, affects the lives of our community. The *Recorder* not only reports the weekly community headlines but also provides editorials, Ponte Vedra news, local school briefs, the classified, community opinions, county government issues, local sports and, last but not least, the "Movers & Shakers" section.

The *Beaches Leader* commemorated in 2003 its fortieth anniversary as the oldest beaches newspaper in Ponte Vedra Beach. *From the* Beaches Leader, *vol. 1, June 27, 2003, Jacksonville Beach, Florida.*

Beaches Leader/Ponte Vedra Leader, Volume No. 1, Friday, June 21, 1963

The information here was drawn from the Beaches Leader, *a* Ponte Vedra Leader *special publication, June 27, 2003.*

In 1963, the *Beaches Leader* associate editor was Frances McCondichie. The *Sun Times*, a paper established in 1979, was purchased by the *Beaches Leader* in 1985. In 1996, the *Ponte Vedra Leader*, a special edition for Ponte Vedra, began to run. The fortieth-anniversary issue of the *Beaches Leader/Ponte Vedra Leader* was released on June 27, 2003. Bob and Ruby Scott were owners from 1963 to 1971. Bill and Beryl Dryden were owners from 1971 to 1983. Tom and Eve Wood were owners from 1983 to 2010.[150]

THE FIRST EDITION NOTE IN 1963: INTRODUCING THE *BEACHES LEADER*

For us—and we hope for you, also—this is an important day. The first issue of the *Beaches Leader* is the fulfillment of a long cherished dream of creating a real "Voice of the People," a newspaper dedicated to presenting all the facts, pro and con, on civic issues; a newspaper helping neighbors, to become better acquainted with each other; a newspaper advocating understanding and teamwork as the foundation of progress; and a newspaper serving the best interests of individuals, business and government. These are lofty goals and some may call them impractical, but they encompass the deals upon which our nation was founded and upon which the survival of true democracy is dependent.[151]

Like Topsy, our Beaches have grown and grown and are still growing. We believe the time has come to give broader coverage than a single newspaper can provide in a community so filled with activity. By adding our facility to those media of communication already in existence, we hope to broaden the general interest in all matters affecting our residents and to become a builder with them of a finer future for all.

Robert L. Scott
Editor—Publisher

THE FIRST EDITION NOTE IN 1969: INTRODUCING THE *PONTE VEDRA RECORDER*

We'll never make the professional golf circuit!

We'll never paint the great American masterpiece!

We'll never write the great American novel!

But maybe, just maybe, with everybody's help, we can do something really worthwhile. So, this announces the inevitable Happening in our life…the birth of the first Ponte Vedra newspaper, dedicated to accurate coverage of events taken place in our Community that so often pass unnoticed.

As Ponte Vedra has grown over the past few years it has become increasingly obvious that some sort of community communication was desirable for all of us who make up this wonderful, unusual bit of Heaven located on the northeastern coast of Florida.

Ponte Vedra is replete with interesting people who have done and are doing fascinating things, making real news for all of us.

New families join us, others move away…loved ones pass on, grandchildren arrive…young men serve our Country in many capacities, sons and daughters go off to institutions of higher learning…golf and tennis enthusiasts plan for competitive programs, the swim teams win trophies and ribbons…young scouts and brownies learn by doing…and on and on…the Fireman's ball, the Christmas party, the Community Association charitable drives…all make Ponte Vedra news.

In the months and years to come, the *Ponte Vedra Recorder*, hopefully, will be eagerly anticipated by all of you. In time you may fondly nickname it "The Wreck," which would be just fine with us! You'll find friends and relatives away from home will welcome it. Regular Colony summer and winter residents who consider Ponte Vedra their second home will enjoy keeping in touch.

We urge your full cooperation in patronizing the very select group of commercial contributors to the *Ponte Vedra Recorder*. It is YOUR newspaper, and only YOU can make it go and grow!

Please keep us fully informed concerning any "happening" you feel would interest any part of the community. The *Recorder* will be published semi-monthly, and sold on an annual subscription basis. This schedule should make it possible to fill each edition with worthwhile news. We welcome all the help you can give us.

To be successful and enduring the *Recorder* must be a full Community effort.

Gretchen Carpenter, Editor and Publisher
Peg Bradford, Associate Editor

South Ponte Vedra Beach

1920s to present

The Road to South Ponte Vedra Beach (SPV)

Picture the land without a road and without a single house—all virgin land from the dunes to the marsh as far as the eye could see, covered with palmettos, sea oats, sawgrass and other vegetation associated with this area. This is what the land running from Guana to north of Vilano Beach must have looked like until 1927, when St. Johns County gave a contract to the B.B. McCormick Company to cut through the dunes and to clear and grade the land for a road. Inna Heilman, the local association historian, was told that Mr. McCormick stood there and personally established the alignment of the road.

Clearing the land must have been very hard work in those still primitive times. Men, mules and slip pans, forerunners of modern road-building equipment, did the work. Since the mules needed water, two artesian wells were drilled, one north of SPV and one across from the gate station. The water from these wells was good water, but it was smelly due to its high sulfur content. Both wells were capped during the 1980s to stop wasting the continually flowing water typical for artesian wells.

The first phase of the road-building project just included grading and took about two years to complete (1927–30). When the State of Florida designated the road as a state road, it also took over the financial responsibility. The B.B. McCormick Company was chosen again to complete and pave the road. After some experimentation with oyster shells and other materials, limestone was chosen as the best material for the roadbed. The paving was finally completed in about 1930.

The paving of the road from Ponte Vedra Beach to Vilano Beach was completed by 1932, thus permitting easier access. But when World War II began, the land south of Mickler's was still uninhabited, except or a few scattered shacks. This was the beginning. It opened up the area we now call South Ponte Vedra Beach.

WHAT IS "SOUTH PONTE VEDRA BEACH"?

South Ponte Vedra Beach covers the area along the beach from Guana Park to Vilano Beach and from the Atlantic Ocean to the Intracoatal Waterway (North River). Although SPV has been lengthened a few times as a result of development, it still sits north of its neighbors in Vilano Beach, North Beach and Usina Beach.

Since they are related by name to Ponte Vedra Beach, let's begin by first reading a little about our neighbor to the north. In 1947, Stockton, Whatley, Davin & Company (SWD) proceeded with plans to develop a strip of land between the ocean and A1A stretching five and a half miles toward the north from the SPV Park. The land was divided into 262 plots, with some deed restrictions calling for single-family houses only. The lots were sold to individual owners. The new community was named South Ponte Vedra Beach.

Stockton, Whatley, Davin & Company, the owner of the Guana area, has not only respected our desire to know more information but has also always listened to our concerns and tried to help whenever and wherever possible. A case in point was the effort to prevent driving over the dunes north of SPV by bringing in truckloads of stones and concrete. When the time came to build the fire station (and again when we wanted to enlarge it to have it become our community center), SWD donated sufficient land for the building and parking. In return, Volunteer Fire Station 9 fought quite a few brush fires over the years on what was then SWD land.

South Ponte Vedra was a very small community when the South Ponte Vedra Association Inc. (SPVA) began with a group of citizens in 1971. Only eighty houses had been built—mostly small concrete block beach cottages and a few framed houses on stilts in between. There was a lot of open land in SPV, but there were very few permanent residents. Many owners lived in Jacksonville and used their houses for weekend relaxation "to get away from it all."

Unfortunately, at times, burglaries were rampant and spoiled the fun. It became obvious that no one in St. Johns County knew of our existence except for the tax collector. That is why twenty-six families founded the South Ponte Vedra Association on June 24, 1972, at the Guana Dam area. The first meeting of the small group of citizens and neighbors in the area was held at the U.S. Coast Guard Station. The driving forces for the association were Richard Oldenburg and Larry Picus.[152]

The SPVA had goals of better police protection, beach vehicular traffic control and protection of the environment. The group quickly bonded into a cohesive civic and social organization. In 1974, the association voted to organize and maintain a volunteer fire department for the area. Over the years, the association has built and expanded a volunteer fire department building, adding an activities center and an outdoor deck in addition to the residence for the fire chief.[153]

SPV's Fire Department

On June 21, 1975, the first fire chief for the volunteer fire station in South Ponte Vedra Beach was Emory Torrey, who was also president of the area's neighborhood association. The first fire captain was Doug Vanderbilt. The first fire engine was purchased in June 1975 from Annapolis, Maryland; it was driven down by Fire Coordinator Bob Jones. Building plans proceeded during that time.

Contributions of coats, boots, miscellaneous equipment and a stretcher have been donated by St. Johns County. Mr. Frank Usina had cleared the land for the new firehouse and the necessary fill. In November 1981, two separate developers requested the rezoning of the eighty-six acres adjacent to the SPV Park. The two developers withdrew their rezoning petitions; the option on the property ran out and reverted back to the owners, the Goodwin brothers, who submitted plans for lots for single-family houses. The Goodwins sold the land to Charlie Brown, who named it Turtle Shores.

Until 1982, South Ponte Vedra Beach was a community of five and a half miles that ended at the SPV Park. When extensive development south of the park began, the U.S. Post Office made the decision to include all developments up to the new bend in the road into the mail delivery district of Ponte Vedra. Thus, Turtle Shores became zip code 32082 and a part of South Ponte Vedra Beach.

U.S. Coast Guard Station and the Old Store

The "Old" U.S. Coast Guard Station was built where the gate station is now, providing quarters for the men and stables for the horses, which were assigned to the daily horse patrols along the beach. This two-story wooden building on SWD land was set on a bluff and was also used as an observation and weather station.[154]

The Coast Guard Station sat on a parcel of land located on the east shore of Matanzas Inlet, facing A1A and the ocean. Coast Guard personnel, accompanied by dogs, maintained a horseback patrol along the coast until they erected lookout towers on the beach. The towers were situated at the dune line, five miles apart, and were manned around the clock for the duration of World War II.[155]

The Old Store was a building erected by Stockton, Whatley, Davin & Company in the 1930s and was used as a surfer station. "Sandpounders" patrolled the beach area with dogs and horses. When World War II broke out, SWD leased the building to the U.S. Navy for one dollar per year, and it became a Coast Guard Station. There was no electric power then, and water was stored in a wooden tank on a tower behind the building. That water came from the old well across the road that furnished cool refreshment to motorists and picnickers. It was sunk many years ago to water the mules that the McCormick Company used to haul labor and equipment through the palmettos as they cut a road south from the beaches along the ocean.

Following the war, the building reverted back to SWD and was temporarily closed, but repeated acts of vandalism made it necessary to have someone on the premises, and Robert J. Henson of Palm Valley arrived with his wife, Ava, in the spring of 1947. They installed a kitchen, used a truck with pulley lines to ground the old water tower in the rear, hooked up the well across the road and settled down for five years. In 1949, a store stocked with merchandise was installed, and it became known as the Old Store.

Mr. Henson indicated that shortly after he arrived he checked the channels in the Guano River, which flowed directly behind the building, at the request of Mr. Brown Whatley, then president of the Ponte Vedra Corporation. Finding the river navigable (the shallow depth at low tide was seven feet), channel markers were placed, and Mr. Whatley was the first yacht owner to tie up at the newly installed one-hundred-foot-long dock.

Henson recalled the many summer weekends when the Jacksonville Yacht Club tied up its pleasure boats for long weekends, holding fish fries on the property. He also remembered the Cuban 110-foot yacht that tied up at the dock for two nights, as well as the three northbound yachts from Melbourne, Florida, whose passengers came by and stayed to watch the coronation of Queen Elizabeth on the Hensons' brand-new television set.

During Mr. Henson's five-year residence at the old store, young Ebbie LeMaster (later manager of the Pont Vedra Club) spent several summers there. Fresh out of school, this was to be Ebbie's first real venture in the real estate business. He loved the area and spent his summers showing oceanfront property to prospective customers, selling ready-built homes for the corporation as well.

Lots were selling for $975 for a seventy-five-foot frontage on the ocean and $1,300 for one hundred feet. Finished one-bedroom homes were $7,000. When not working, Ebbie spent his leisure hours hunting, fishing and enjoying the ocean, and he and the Hensons became lifelong friends.

Robert Henson also reminisced about the winter of 1950, when he awoke one morning to find two inches of snow on the ground, the palmettos blanketed as far as the eye could see. He also remembered the hurricane of 1950, when the sand drifts caused by ninety-five-mile-per-hour winds so disguised the road that motorists, thinking that they had already left the road, drove off into the wilderness.

During the early years, a weather station was maintained on the premises. After the Hensons moved back to Palm Valley, a new superintendent was hired. With the able assistance of Postmaster Alice Landrum, a substation post office was installed, with one window to serve the customers. Mr. Henson also remembered that Mr. Whatley at one time worked with the wildlife officials at the Game and Freshwater Fish Commission to determine if it would be practical to plant oyster beds in the Guano River. At that time, there was no dam. It was decided that the pollution from the boats would not make this feasible, and the idea was discarded.

The story was continued by Joe (Edward) DeGrove, the next proprietor, who arrived in 1963 and who also was a native of Palm Valley. Joe lived at the store with his wife, Lavelle, as well as Sharon and Russell, two of their six children. When Joe and Lavelle took over the Old Store, the post office having been closed, they removed the "cubbyhole" from the store. Sometime after the powerful Hurricane Dora passed through, a pool table, a pinball machine and a ten-pin game were installed in the old storage room.

For security reasons, the DeGrove family resided there most of the time, although they also maintained an oceanfront home about a mile down the road. The DeGroves, at that time, had two bedrooms, a living room, a dining area and a family kitchen, all of which had been added to the original building. Besides tending the store, Joe operated the weather station, sending the coiled information from the barometer every fourth day—and the wind velocity cylinder information every fourteen days—to the U.S. Weather Bureau in Jacksonville. Before Dora, the outdoor weather equipment adorned the top of the peaked roof, but it was later installed on a pole beside the highway. When the Guano Dam was built directly north of the Old Store, the area was regarded as a waterfowl reserve, and no license was required for fishing.

This area is probably one of the few fishing spots in the United States, at this time, where freshwater fishing is contiguous to saltwater fishing. Guano River, behind the Old Store, is salt water, and the river above the dam, which extends about ten miles, is pure water for the first six miles and brackish for the next four.

Hurricane Dora's destructive force and extensive damage to one of the houses on the beach in South Ponte Vedra Beach in 1964. *From the Beaches Area Historical Society Collection.*

The store was used as headquarters for law enforcement officials, civil defense personnel and conservation employees, all of whom were housed there and on constant duty for thirty-six hours during the height of one storm. Incredible as it may seem, law enforcement officers worked on two-hour shifts around the clock apprehending people who were carrying off refrigerators, radios, television sets or anything they could lift from the oceanfront homes in the area that had been evacuated. During Dora, eighteen homes were severely damaged, and twelve more disappeared into the ocean, but the Old Store, rugged and weather-beaten, solid as the land on which it still stands, gave up only a few shingles and a few leaks from the roof.

In the 1970s, as the area north and south of the Old Store grew at an incredible rate, it was hoped that the South Ponte Vedra Store would not succumb to the demolition block. As progress took place and a new gate station was built, pictures of the Old Store still bring a pang of nostalgia for the old-timers, as well as a reminder to all newcomers that some things were around there for a long, long time.[156]

The year 1980 seemed to be the endless summer. The signs of fall were just a little subtle that year, but they were there. On calm days, one could see large dark-green patches moving south in an emerald-green ocean. Those were the mullets on their way south. The tides were getting higher, especially during full moon. The wind came more readily from the northeast and churned up the ocean.

THE BEACHING OF THE *ROCKET*

It was just such a northeaster that brought the big news to the beach in the form of the *Rocket*. The eighty-five-foot converted navy ship was owned by missionaries, who were taking supplies to one of the hurricane-stricken islands

The beaching of a tanker ship in 1947 during a storm on the shores of South Ponte Vedra Beach. *From the Beaches Area Historical Society Collection.*

down south. Instead, they ran into engine trouble. During the night of August 25, 1980, the ship was stranded. It became evident very quickly that any efforts to pull the ship out to sea would fail. The ship had broken into two parts. The work of the Coast Guard and the force of the ocean during high tide had reduced the size of the two sections considerably. It was sad to see a once proud ship disintegrate on South Ponte Vedra shores.

In August 1983, the Texas Holding Company of SWD decided to sell the entire Guana area, including the four miles of beach property north of SPV. The buyer was Gate Land Company of Jacksonville, owned by Herb Peyton. In March 1984, permission was granted by St. Johns County to Herb Peyton to build the two-story convenience store with a gas station on the land of the old Coast Guard Station.

The South Ponte Vedra Beach volunteer fire department, located next to the gate station, has changed. The physical location of the fire station was moved farther south, still on the west side of A1A but next to Turtle Shores, across from the public entrance to the beach. It is now operated by paid firefighters from St. Johns County.

It wasn't very long (1984 in fact) before the governor of Florida gave approval to purchase the Guana area under the Conservation and Recreation Land (CARL) program. The state was also considering including the land adjacent to the south owned by the Goodwins and Auburn University, which was a tract west of A1A that was zoned for quadruplex units.

SERENATA BEACH

How did this area of Ponte Vedra come up with the musical name of "Serenata"? The Roman version of the name was more connected to friends and family celebrations or to an unstaged vocal performance with backdrops.

The Serenata Beach Club in South Ponte Vedra Beach began development in about 2000 with flagship condominium units on the Intracoastal Waterway. *Serenata Beach Club, 2012, Jane Norton, general manager.*

Serenatas, or serenate, were a form of eighteenth-century vocal music—like a cantata, oratorio or opera—but shorter, simpler and unpretentious. They were written to commemorate special occasions. After seeing and visiting Serenata Beach, you will know exactly why the name was chosen because it will be like music to your ears and eyes, just like one of Handel's serenatas.

The southern end of Ponte Vedra Beach again moved its dividing line farther south of Turtle Shores in 1999, when renowned Ponte Vedra developer Paul Fletcher, Jaguars owner Tom Petway and Pittsburgh multibillionaire Henry Hillman got involved. When Serenata Beach Condo/Townhomes, Ocean Villas of Serenata and Ocean Grande of Serenata (west of A1A) began building on each side of A1A, the southern end of Ponte Vedra Beach was extended that short distance into Vilano Beach to include the name Ponte Vedra Beach.

When plans for Serenata Beach started coming together in 1999, the $160 million condominium and clubhouse project had the backing of some impressive corporate headliners like Fletcher, Petway and Hillman. Putting upscale condominium homes and a clubhouse on the last beachfront stretch of South Ponte Vedra Beach (a sacred fifty-acre parcel long held by the Davis family's DDI Inc., which bought it from a bank that foreclosed on a former owner) was an investment hard to pass up.

"The reason we became so enamored with the site is that from every direction, the views are truly spectacular," Fletcher said. Now that Serenata Beach is coming out of the sand, the project is catching the attention of some less well-known but equally celebrated investors: home buyers. And they're not just trickling in. Condo buyers at the South Ponte Vedra development are crashing in like tidal waves.

The 90-unit Ocean Villas at the Serenata Beach portion of the development sold out quickly. The construction, which was completed in 2007, on the Ocean Grande at the Serenata Beach development across State Road A1A from Flagship's condominiums, was the final stage. The Ocean Grande project now includes 206 three-bedroom condominiums units on the Intracoastal Waterway.[157]

HOW HAS THE SPV AREA CHANGED?

Today, many of the homes that were built on the beach have been converted back into rental properties rather than residential year-round homes, which changed the complexion of the remaining permanent South Ponte Vedra residents.[158]

Even with the many changes that have taken place recently in South Ponte Vedra Beach—with the Serenata development, more beach homes converted to rentals, the extensive expansion of the Guana area and the million-dollar price tags on many homes—the citizens who first began living in this area of the beach can still recall the many interesting events of the past.[159]

Vicar's Landing

1980s

Why Is Vicar's Landing Unique?

Vicar's Landing is a life care retirement community dedicated to providing superior healthcare services, if needed, to its members. The groundbreaking was held on January 5, 1987, and it first opened in 1988.

Vicar's Landing is owned and operated by Life Care Pastoral Services Inc. (LCPS), which was established by members of Christ Episcopal Church in Ponte Vedra Beach. LCPS is a not-for-profit organization and is not affiliated with any religious organization. Vicar's is the only life care retirement community within Ponte Vedra Beach and is located within the Sawgrass Community.

In 1982, Christ Church formed a committee and decided to sponsor a committee to investigate a life care center in the Ponte Vedra area. The committee learned three things. First, the best life care facilities are physically very attractive and have convenient support facilities. Second, "life care" means that from the time you enter as an ambulatory but not necessarily healthy person, you will be taken care of for the rest of your life. And finally, "life care" represents a very serious kind of insurance. Vicar's would require a substantial down payment and a monthly fee and would always insure against the possible costs of nursing home care.

Peter Rummell, general manager of Arvida, became interested in locating the proposed life care facility at the Tournament Players Championship (TPC) site a few hundred yards inside the Sawgrass Community gate.[160] In 1985, Reverend James Cooper noted the early history of the Vicar's project: "In the early '80s, a committee of Christ Church studied family life and aging and became aware of a need for retirement care living in the community."

Funds were sought to finance the initial marketing, preliminary design and development costs. KBJ, a well-known local architectural firm, was engaged on October 21, 1985, to generate preliminary design and development data from which plans could be shown to potential clients for marketing purposes. Vicar's Landing was then designed as a picturesque twenty-four-acre coastal campus community with proximity to existing golf courses, the oceanfront and resort facilities, including a community center and a lake within the exclusive gated community of Sawgrass.

The purpose of Vicar's Landing is to provide a setting where older people can continue living independently for as long as possible while ensuring that excellent healthcare, companionship and support services will always be immediately at hand. In 1988, Vicar's Landing began as a private, nonprofit venture undertaken as a result of individual and church interest and initiative.[161]

VICAR'S LANDING'S MISSION

Vicar's mission statement reads:

> *The mission of Life Care Pastoral Services, Inc. is to provide retirement communities of superior quality to those individuals who entrust us with their future health, social, spiritual and recreational needs and who wish to continue the standard of living they previously enjoyed…We shall strive to provide our complement of services, supportive and attractive atmosphere through dedicated professionals. Respect and empathy for the individuality, privacy and independence of our members are of paramount importance.*

A write-up on Vicar's Landing continued:

> *Life at Vicar's Landing is as active—or as laid back—as you want it to be. Vicar's offers an abundance of activities in a resort-oriented, life-care community. The Northeast Florida location makes this an outstanding setting for outdoor activities, with a refreshing, mild change of seasons. Their staff understand that their residents seek personal fulfillment, independence and an invigorating lifestyle. And that's just what they offer, in an atmosphere of casual elegance.*
>
> *You will find a wide range of exquisite accommodations on their picturesque 24-acre campus. All housing features fully equipped electric kitchens, elevators and available guest accommodations.*
>
> *Whether you choose a patio home or an apartment, you will enjoy maintenance-free living, with everything you need nearby. Situated in*

> *one of the most desirable communities of Florida's east coast, they offer beautiful year-round weather, a quiet but vibrant community, and a wealth of amenities and attractions.*

Vicar's is proud that its residents have a strong voice in governing Vicar's Landing, with representation on the board of directors. The board, and its entire organization, strives diligently to offer the finest possible lifestyle.

The best time to move to Vicar's Landing is when you are in good health. This ensures that your healthcare facilities are provided without additional cost. Vicar's operates under only the highest standards of ethics. Also, you can enjoy a wide array of recreational activities both on campus and off. Moving when you feel healthy results in opportunities to make new friendships. Many members say, "We wish we had done this earlier…Don't wait too long."

MEMBER EXPERIENCES

Robert P.T. Young's article in the *Ponte Vedra Recorder* in 1985 emphasized the importance of deciding to start Vicar's Landing. Young relayed the story of a Ponte Vedra couple that had a powerful effect on him. When Robert P.T. and Harriet Young were considering moving to Vicar's Landing back in 1985, Harriet could not decide, thinking that Vicar's would be just another first-class retirement home. Robert finally made his decision when the wife of his friend Frank Clarke got sick, was hospitalized in Jacksonville and died at home. Later, Frank himself got sick and died in a nursing home in Jacksonville. Robert decided that the most important Christian mission that might be accomplished in the parish would be to find a way to maintain or perhaps even improve the standard of living of the citizens as they grow older.

The culmination of years of effort went into the planning of Vicar's Landing. Condominiums were built in a magnificently landscaped area in an ideal, safe and beautiful location. Sawgrass has done a truly outstanding job of maintaining the quality of its neighborhoods, and Vicar's Landing has more than met these standards.

Robert and Harriet learned in 1985 that moving from a large house to any condominium requires the sacrifice of some furniture and possessions. The Youngs discovered that they could select and take along their most cherished and important possessions. When they finally moved to Vicar's, they both were impressed with the three meals in the dining room, including cocktails, and that the significant part of the governance of Vicar's Landing is vested in the Residents' Committee.[162]

One of the most interesting features designed by the residents of Vicar's was the introduction of younger folks to serve the meals. One of the best ways for the residents to stay young was to request that young girls and boys serve the evening meals. This became beneficial to both. The residents felt more youthful and, in return, donated scholarship funds to many of the servers each year.

Vicar's Landing is a close-knit community of friends and neighbors who welcome the opportunity to participate in the numerous programs and events. There is always an interesting variety of events to choose from if you want to be involved in community recreational and educational opportunities. The pleasures and privileges of retirement at its best are evident every day at Vicar's Landing at Sawgrass. It is a beautiful facility for people who want to share their lives with one another and enjoy dining in the company of youths.

The Cultural Center

The Cultural Center at 50 Executive Way, Ponte Vedra Beach, is the heart and soul of the Ponte Vedra community. It continues to offer art exhibits and shows, lectures, concerts and a range of diversified classes every six weeks. The center urges your family and friends to call regarding membership opportunities.

The Cultural Center is the central place where Ponte Vedra residents of all ages learn, play and experience the arts. It is open to the public. Many of its programs are offered at little to no charge. The goal of the Cultural Center is to offer broad public access to a wide variety of art, cultural education and lifelong learning. The center is a nonprofit organization that provides needed enrichment opportunities to the community and depends on the community for support.

The center's mission statement reads: "To enhance the lives of the Northeast Florida community by fostering and developing the visual and performing arts and by offering a variety of educational opportunities at The Cultural Center's new facility in Ponte Vedra Beach."

Founded in 1994 by a dedicated group of community leaders, the Ponte Vedra Cultural Center began in 1996 and was temporally located on the east side of A1A across from the Fairfield/Azalea Point Subdivision. The center was then moved to a nicer and larger building on Executive Way, where it remains today.

Executive Director Dick Williams said, "We are proud to be the largest cultural arts facility in St. Johns County, Florida. Our eight-thousand-square-foot facility houses a wonderful art gallery with exhibitions that feature local and regional artists. In addition to our gallery, the Cultural Center provides studio facilities for our art, dance, music and voice instruction classes. Most importantly, the Cultural Center provides a unique gathering place for everyone in our community to create, understand and experience the arts."

The Cultural Center has made its permanent home here in a location that was formerly the U.S. Post Office after moving from a smaller location farther south on A1A. *Photo by M. Robinson, 2008.*

The Cultural Center is living its dream of journeying toward artistic excellence by nurturing local talent in the community. Ponte Vedra Beach has been enriched culturally and economically through the development of the center. It enhances the quality of life and improves the caliber of education throughout the area. Additionally, it has stimulated visitation to St. Johns County and further positive economic development.

History has shown that a community can only be truly great when it allows the arts to flourish. Ponte Vedra and the Cultural Center together will make for a creative powerhouse for generations to come. The Cultural Center has "Sculpted Our Community" in four phases:

Phase I—A Strong Structure in an Ideal Location
Acquired the U.S. Post Office complex and existing structure

Phase II—An Exhibition Gallery
Traveling art collections and regional exhibits
Gallery to produce art shows for talent in the area
Functional home for musical presentations and art exhibits

Phase III—A Magnificent Exterior
A sculpture garden entrance
Capacity and parking

Phase IV—A State-of-the-Art Facility
State-of-the-art equipment
A sculpture studio
Program development

The jewel has been set in Ponte Vedra's cultural crown. The arts are a catalyst for change, and the entire community is enhanced when everyone becomes involved—not just with the soaring spirit of the arts but also with the practice and discipline of creating it. This plan has been fueled by unprecedented philanthropy from a few visionary corporations, organizations and individuals. Through the arts, the Cultural Center not only helps ensure that Ponte Vedra is a culturally richer place in which to live, work and raise our children but also ensures that we continue to be recognized as a vibrant and prosperous community.

The Cultural Center is a place where ordinary, day-to-day concerns can be left behind and the imagination can be set free. The opportunity to showcase and perpetuate the names of our honored benefactors within such an institution is rare. As guests pause during their visits to our exhibits, they

These beach scenes are inviting for a day on the beach and for the artists who paint these beautiful sights on canvas. *Photo by Ellen Diamond, 2012.*

will also peruse the names ascribed to the walls, galleries and studios. Few will be aware of the years of effort preceding the construction of this landmark. They will only experience a magnificent treasure.

Artist Ellen Diamond, who allowed one of her beach paintings to be used on the cover of my first book and this book, offers the Ellen Diamond Workshop through the Cultural Center and is a huge success. Ellen also has an artist workshop that she conducts annually in northern Italy.

Hayes Memorial Arts Kids Scholarship Fund

The Cultural Center, in conjunction with the *Ponte Vedra Recorder*, announced the formation of the Grace Hayes Memorial Arts for Kids Scholarship Fund, which will provide scholarships for area underserved children ages four through fourteen to attend a variety of art classes and camps at the Cultural Center.

The Arts for Kids Fund was created as a way to pay tribute to Grace Hayes for her lifetime dedication to the service of others. Grace Hayes played many important roles in our community, as the editor of the *Ponte Vedra Recorder* and by serving on a multitude of community service boards and committees.

In addition to the exceptional on-site programming, the center offers a wide scope of educational opportunities for underserved communities throughout the beaches and St. Johns County. Our center's outreach efforts are targeted at reaching children and adults by bringing high-quality arts education and artistic experiences to community centers, rehabilitation centers and special-needs schools.

Volunteers

The Cultural Center is always seeking great volunteers who are looking for opportunities to connect with others in the community. Volunteers are rewarded by the experience of working in a fun, creative and lovely environment. They also have the satisfaction of knowing that their donation of talent and time helps us reach more in our community.

The center has recently created a new volunteer organization dedicated to supporting the needs and mission of the Cultural Center and the arts. It is truly the place in our community to create, understand and experience the arts. It accomplishes this through exhibitions of local, regional and national artists in a variety of media; through exciting events for the community; and through quality art classes, lectures and workshops. The Cultural Center has gained a reputation as a gem in the regional arts community, and it is proud of that!

Nocatee

West of the Intracoastal

Location

This area of Nocatee, west of the Intracoastal Waterway, was an extension of Palm Valley, accessible over the Mickler Palm Valley bridge—and a place where a significant change has taken place. This area, now called Nocatee, contains historic areas that were discussed in the earlier Palm Valley history.

Nocatee, in the past, contained sites such as Twenty Mile Station or Halfway House; La Casa de Los Dragones; the train that stopped at Durbin station; that dirt road named Highway Number 1; School No. 27, established in 1883 at Twenty Mile Ridge in Durbin; the Oesterreicher homestead (still standing), back in the 1800s; and a few sawmills on the west banks of the Intracoastal.

Of course, I have to mention the log cabin, Fort Davis, built by the Stocktons (and purchased later by the Davises), as well as, finally, the moonshine production in the 1900s.

The Davises

The Davis family, founders of the Winn-Dixie supermarket chain, put their land, time and efforts into a massive undertaking to ensure the legacy of the family name: Nocatee, a fourteen-thousand-acre mixed-use development slated for St. Johns County and a small part of Duval County that had plans to break ground in 2005 and happened right on time.

"But housing doesn't scratch the surface of the proposed Nocatee development. Nocatee has become its own town, with its own zip code, and will take twenty-five years to be considered at 'fully built-out,'" said Richard Ray, then chairman of the Tolomato district.

Because Nocatee straddles two counties (about 15 percent of the community is in Duval), two community development districts—special-purpose local governments that were re-created and governed by Florida statues—have been established. The Tolomato and Split Pine Community Development Districts, which encompass all of Nocatee, were approved by the Florida Land & Water Adjudicatory Commission in July 2004.

Fort Davis was built in 1942 by James Roosevelt Stockton Sr., who named it the "Haunt of the Hermit." The Davises bought the house and twenty-acre property in 1954 and renamed the house Dee-Dot, which is still standing today among the Nocatee development. *From* Dee-Dot Ranch and Twenty Mile House: A History, *Jacksonville University Archives, Jacksonville, Florida.*

This extensive tract of land (fifteen thousand acres) and master development required a unique landowner, and the Davises were just that. The Davis family sold most of the Nocatee property to the developers. "It requires patience, commitment, time and capital. It has taken us eight years to get this far," said Richard Ray. "This is a comprehensive project that has been master planned. It was the Davis family's thought that instead of selling the land piecemeal, they would leave behind a legacy and embark on the master plan to create a sustainable community, one where families can live, work and play."[163]

Further contributions made to the community and northeast Florida included nearly $150 million in regional roadway improvements from the Intracoastal Bridge to U.S. 1 that replaced the two-lane County Road 210.

NOCATEE GOUNDBREAKING

After its announcement in March 1999, the Nocatee development began to get underway. The first groundbreaking began in October 2005. Even though the majority of the development, including most of the fifteen thousand residential housing units and the population of about thirty thousand, will be south of the rerouted SR 210, some of the development will be located in what was called Ponte Vedra Beach.

However, it was not long before Nocatee requested zoning and reclassification of the area to be called "Ponte Vedra," with a separate zip code. When this was approved, Nocatee began to be called Ponte Vedra without "Beach" at the end. Nocatee was planned as an alternative to the rampant development that typically overwhelms high-growth areas.

As part of the development order for the fifteen-thousand-home, fifteen-thousand-acre community, the Parc Group agreed to donate several land sites for nine public schools, two fire stations and the preserve, which has three and a half miles of frontage along the Intracoastal Waterway. The land also provides a buffer that will be one to one and a half miles wide between the waterway and the future developments in Nocatee's commercial and residential areas.

NOCATEE PRESERVE

The Nocatee Preserve encompasses 2,400 acres of wildly beautiful land fronting a three-and-a-half-mile stretch of the Intracoastal Waterway known as the Tolomato River. Donated to St. Johns County for use as a public park for passive recreation, the Nocatee Preserve is a rare conservation area of undisturbed old Florida flora and fauna. This kind of nature-smart planning does more than guarantee our native wildlife residents a safe haven. It guarantees all of us the wonder of hiking, biking and bird watching in their company for generations to come.

Nocatee's High School

Ponte Vedra High School (PVHS) is the public high school in the St. Johns County School District, located in Nocatee in northeast St. Johns County. The high school was constructed in 2009 to relieve overcrowding at Allen Nease Senior High School on U.S. Route 1 about eight miles away, although it is still within the area called Ponte Vedra.

Although PVHS is located in Nocatee near the Intracoastal Waterway, the school is zoned for the community of Ponte Vedra Beach. Nease High School, also in Ponte Vedra, is known for academic excellence and football, with Tim Tebow going on to be the star player with the University of Florida Gators.

Nocatee Communities

No matter what type or size of new home and neighborhood you're looking for, you're sure to find it in Nocatee. Each of the village-like neighborhoods has its own personality, offering a variety of beautiful homes—single-family homes, luxury estate homes, condominiums and town homes—all built by some of Florida's finest home builders.

Nocatee's variety of neighborhoods range from the intimate to the expansive, each with its own character, gathering places and amenities. There are communities for adults ages fifty-five and older, and many are suited for growing families. Singles, couples, children, seniors…together at home in this new coastal community called Nocatee.

Today there are eight different and unique communities that make up the Nocatee community: Greenleaf Village, Kelly Pointe, Enclave at Town Center, Austin Park, Coastal Oaks, Willowcove, Del Webb Ponte Vedra and Tidewater.

Two of the unique communities that must be mentioned in detail are the Del Webb Ponte Vedra and Enclave at Town Center.

Del Webb Ponte Vedra

For anyone age fifty-five and older who has ever longed to live near the ocean, Del Webb proudly presents Del Webb Ponte Vedra at Nocatee. Located in the prestigious Ponte Vedra area between Jacksonville and St. Augustine, this is Florida at its best, with active adult living at its finest. Del Webb Ponte Vedra provides a gated community within the award-winning Nocatee master plan, conveniently located just minutes off the ocean but also near dining, shopping and recreation. Adjoining Del Webb Ponte Vedra is the Nocatee preserve, 2,400 wildly beautiful acres along the Intracoastal Waterway offering a variety of outdoor sites and activities.

Del Webb Ponte Vedra itself encompasses more than 1,014 coastal Florida acres. Gated and private, the community's master plan envisions about 1,988 residences centered on the vast and vibrant array of amenities and recreational venues that are the hallmarks of the renowned Del Webb active adult lifestyle. Homes in Del Webb Ponte Vedra are designed with beautiful architecture and include single-family and low-maintenance carriage homes.

The scale of the amenities planned for Del Webb Ponte Vedra sets the lifestyle pace for a community of this scope and stature. Recently opened, the thirty-seven-thousand-square-foot Anastasia Club at Del Webb Ponte Vedra is the perfect setting for residents to socialize with friends and neighbors and offers indoor and outdoor pools, a state-of-the-art fitness center, arts and crafts facilities, multipurpose rooms, a social café, a grand ballroom with a stage and outdoor courts for tennis, bocce ball and pickleball. Residents will also enjoy Central Park, as well as covered picnic pavilions, nature trails and more than six miles of walking and biking trails.

Enclave at Town Center

The first Town Center neighborhood, Enclave at Town Center, offers an opportunity to live in a way that puts the environment on a higher pedestal. Created with sustainability and environmental stewardship at its core, the new Enclave at Town Center will offer contemporary and energy-efficient urban designs in a location where you can enjoy a walk or bike ride to local amenities like the Splash Water Park or the shops in Town Center.

Notes

Guana's Human Habitation

1. Guana Tolomato Matanzas National Estuarine Research Reserve Management Plan, December 2008, 23.
2. Ibid., 24.
3. Ibid., 21.
4. Douglas, "Find of Ceremonial Axes," 100–109; Douglas, "Some Characteristics of the Indian Earth and Shell Mounds," 74–82, 140–47.
5. Deagan, Phase I Background Research; Hann, "Summary Guide"; Worth, "Tolomato in the Documentary Record."
6. Worth, "Tolomato in the Documentary Record"; Hann, "Summary Guide."
7. Weisman and Newman, National Register form draft.
8. Schafer, *Oldest City*.
9. Griffin, "Life on the Plantations," 163–88.
10. Schafer, *Oldest City*, 98.
11. Schafer, "Early Plantation Development," 47.
12. Neitz, *Cabbageberries, Duck Feathers and the Tides*, 159.
13. Schafer, *Oldest City*, 99–100.
14. Ibid., chap. 4.
15. Neitz, *Cabbageberries, Duck Feathers and the Tides*, 183.
16. Parker, Shell Bluff National Register Nomination documentation, 2.
17. Neitz, *Cabbageberries, Duck Feathers and the Tides*, 159.
18. Baker, Archaeological Excavations at the Shell Bluff Landing Site.
19. Florida Game and Freshwater Fish Commissison (FGFWFC), 1990. "A Conceptual Managemant Plan for the Guana River Wildlife Management Ares, St. Johns County, Florida," Bureau of Wildlife Management Division of Wildlife, FGFWFC, Tallahasee, Florida.
20. Schafer, "Governor James Grant's Villa," 90.

AFRICAN NAMES AND THE AFRICAN DIASPORA TO NORTH FLORIDA

21. Harley, *Timetables of African-American History.*
22. Franklin and Moss, *From Slavery to Freedom*, 33.
23. Ibid., 32.
24. Ibid., 34.
25. Ibid., 37.
26. Ibid., 41.
27. Voyages Database, "The Trans-Atlantic Slave Trade Database: Assessing the Slave Trade," Emory University, 2009.
28. Ibid.
29. West, *Archaeology of Early Colonial Life*.
30. Franklin and Moss, *From Slavery to Freedom*, 114.
31. West, *Archaeology of Early Colonial Life.*
32. Franklin and Moss, *From Slavery to Freedom*, 137.
33. Windley, "Profile of Runaway Slaves," 27; Porter, "Negroes on the Southern Frontier," 53–78.
34. Black Laws of Virginia, Virginia Code, chap. 5, "Free Persons of Color and Slaves," 94. Actually, there were free Negroes long before this time, although the first legislative reference to them seems to have been in 1668.
35. Black Laws, 37.
36. Franklin and Moss, *From Slavery to Freedom*, 81.
37. Bankole, *Slavery and Medicine.*
38. Adams, *Historical Overview of African American Veterinarians.*
39. Painter, *Sojourner Truth.*
40. Lander and Pritchett, "When to Care."
41. Halperin, "Poor, the Black, and the Marginalized."
42. Green-McKenzie, "Training African-American Residents."
43. Morgan, "Education and Medical Practice."
44. Kenny, "I Can Do the Child No Good."
45. Wall, "Medical Ethics of Dr. J. Marion Sims."
46. Watts, "Race Consciousness."
47. Charatzlitt, "Chronicle of Racism."
48. Barrows and Fingers, "Human Trafficking," 464.
49. Byrd, "Race, Medicine, and Health Care."
50. Hagy, "International Conference on Biomedical Horizons."
51. Halperin, "Poor, the Black, and the Marginalized."
52. William Mayo Fulton's letterbook.
53. Fulton's letterbook, "Fort Rus & Florida," written December 13, 1940.
54. Ibid., 50.
55. The fifth verse of the eleventh chapter of Daniel perplexed many of the Africans, but then the verses thirteen through fifteen, which spoke of victory for the North and the slaves, were dwelled upon: "For the king of the north shall raise another army, greater than before; after some years he shall attack with his large army and

great resources. In those times many shall resist the king of the south, and outlaws of your people shall rise up in fulfillment of vision, but they shall fail. When the king of the north comes, he shall set up siegeworks and take the fortified city by storm. The power of the south troops shall not withstand him, and not even his picked troops shall have the strength to resist." Jones, *Born a Child of Freedom*.

56. By the end of the 1530s, the word had taken on strong connotations of being "fierce," "wild" and "unbroken" and was used primarily to refer to African American runaways and English slaves who came to Spanish territory.
57. The word "slave" first appears in English in about 1290, spelled as *sclave*. The spelling is based on Old French *esclave* from Medieval Latin *sclavus*, "slav, slave," first recorded in about 800. Under slavery, a worker (called "a slave") is compelled to work for another (sometimes called "the master," "marster," "massa" or "slave owner").
58. A related phrase from the time of slavery is *gens de couleur*, a French expression that refers to the free descendants of white French colonists and Africans. The word "slave" refers to people who are treated as the property of another person, household, company, corporation or government ("chattel slavery"). The term is meant to be inclusive, emphasizing common experiences of racism. "People of color" is preferred by both nonwhite and minority.
59. The Spanish used *criollo* to distinguish American-born people of European background from Spanish-born Europeans (*peninsulares*).
60. Like many such words (Cuffy, Rastus and so on), it is a common personal name among U.S. blacks in the slavery days (first found in 1704 in Boston), probably from an African source; compare *Foulah sambo* "Uncle" or a similar Hausa word meaning "second son."
61. These words are mainly derived from Latin roots: "quadroon" is borrowed from Spanish *cuarterón* (ultimately from Latin *quartus*, "fourth"), and "octoroon" is modeled on this, from Latin *octo* "eight" (or, equivalently, Greek *okto*). *Quintus* is Latin for "fifth," but "quintroon" does not follow the same logic—it refers to the generation rather than the racial proportion. The alternative "hexadecaroon," from Greek *hexadeka*, "sixteen," expresses this proportion directly.
62. The word originated from the Romance and Latin languages. The feminine word is *zamba*.
63. "Free people of color" was a phrase especially used in New Orleans and the former Louisiana Territory, where a third class of people developed. In Caribbean and Latin American slave societies, specific terms were used to refer to such mixed-race groups, usually with an attempt at classification by appearance or ancestry. The historical phrase "free people of color" refers to people of African descent during slavery who lived in freedom.
64. Tyson, *Blood Done Sign My Name*.
65. Norrece, *Born a Child of Freedom*, 54.
66. Norrece T. Jones Jr., "Slavery Is a Legal System Facilitating Exploitation of Labor," *Richmond Times-Dispatch*, June 14, 2007, 54; Norrece T. Jones Jr., "Pro-Amnesty Argument Recalls Slave Era," letter to the editor, *Richmond-Times Dispatch*, n.d.

67. Tyson, *Blood Done Sign My Name*, 99.
68. The phrase "African Native Americans" is a neologism referring to people who are of both African American and Native American descent, but it is not a synonym of Black Indians.

JONATHAN DICKINSON'S JOURNEY THROUGH NORTH FLORIDA

69. Philip Hamilton McMillan Memorial Publication Fund, New Haven, Connecticut, Yale Historical Publications, 1945.
70. De Coste, "Suffering of the Shipwrecked Quakers"; O'Sullivan and Lane, *Jonathan Dickenson in the Florida Reader*, 41–42.
71. Jonathan Dickinson's placement of Santa Cruz two or three leagues north of St. Augustine was a case of mistaken identity. He mistook Tolomato for Santa Cruz. Hann, *History of Timucua Indians*.
72. *Jonathan Dickenson's Journey*, 116–17.
73. Miller, *Environmental History of Northeast Florida*; Map 6.6, *Jonathan Dickenson's Journey*.
74. McGoun, *Southeast Florida Pioneers*, 5.

FORT MOSÉ

75. Rivers, *Slavery in Florida*, 50.
76. Colburn and Landers, "Traditions of African American Freedom," 18.
77. Harvey, *America's First City*.
78. Deagan and MacMahon, *Fort Mosé*.
79. The first Fort Mosé only lasted for two years, from 1738 to 1740.
80. McCarthy, *Black Florida*, 257.
81. Landers, "Gracia Real de Santa Teresa de Mosé."
82. Jones and McCarthy, *African Americans in Florida*, 94.
83. Landers, "Gracia Real de Santa Teresa de Mosé."
84. Nolan, "White Man's Burden."
85. Landers, "Gracia Real de Santa Teresa de Mosé."
86. Landers, "The Mosé Site."
87. Nolan, "White Man's Burden," 17.
88. Wilson, "Dr. Bronson and Friends."
89. McCarthy, *Black Florida*, 257.
90. Ibid., 259.
91. The second Fort Mosé lasted from 1752 to 1763 before it was destroyed.
92. Colburn and Landers, *African American Heritage*, chap. 2.
93. Deagan and MacMahon, *Fort Mosé*, 37.
94. Jones and McCarthy, *African Americans in Florida*, 10.
95. Landers, "Gracia Real de Santa Teresa de Mosé," 111.
96. McCarthy, *Black Florida*, 260.

97. Colburn and Landers, *African American Heritage*, chap. 2, 34.
98. Wright, "Dispatches of Spanish Officials."
99. Landers, "Gracia Real de Santa Teresa de Mosé"; Colburn and Landers, *African American Heritage*, chap. 2, 35.
100. Landers, "Free and Slave," 181.

EARLY TRANSPORTATION IN NORTH FLORIDA

101. Boykin, *Ponte Vedra Beach.*
102. Eunice Pit Odom Simms's father, Pit, owned the land that is now the Sawgrass and Marsh Landing developments, running a turpentine farm known as Pit's Still.
103. Chance and Smith, *Cultural Resource Survey.*
104. Heilman, "South Ponte Vedra Beach"; personal interview with Inna Heilman, January 26, 2006.
105. Kathy Cramer, "Where's It Been…Where's It Going," *Ponte Vedra Recorder*, September 2, 2005, Section A-4.
106. *Ponte Vedra Recorder*, September 2, 2005, Section A-5.
107. *Beaches Leader Newcomers Guide*, editor's article, 1995.
108. U.S. A1A could be an extension of a numbering quirk in Florida. When FL 1 was reassigned in 1946, the new grid routing for it paralleled the existing U.S. 1. It was rechristened FL A1A in 1947 to alleviate confusion and to pretend to be a U.S. 1 alternate route. (Highway enthusiasts, also known as "road geeks," refer to it as Atlantic 1 Alternate, even though there is no evidence that was the intent.) There is no single highway number stretching along the Atlantic coast as U.S. 101 does along the Pacific coast. U.S. 1, U.S. 9, U.S. 13 and U.S. 17 each come close at times to being true Atlantic coast highways.
109. U.S. Department of Transportation, Federal Highway Administration, National Scenic Byways Program, Washington, D.C.
110. Adams, "The King's Road," 94.
111. Ibid.
112. Historic Properties Survey, Flagler County, Florida, November 1987.
113. Ryan, *Search for Old King's Road*, 36.
114. Droz, *South Atlantic Coastal Highway* map, based heavily on a 1925 Rand McNally map of Florida.
115. Ibid. The *Auto Trails* maps are wonderful records of a time when automobile travel was new and somewhat adventurous.
116. Any segment of U.S. 1 or Old Dixie Highway along the route was probably Atlantic Highway; it also could be referred to as "Atlantic Coastal Highway" extending north to Maine, as "Eastern Coastal Highway" or as "Coastal Highway" along the East Coast.
117. Droz, *South Atlantic Coastal Highway* map.
118. Droz, with Carroll, *Florida Auto Trails.*

Second Spanish Period in North Florida

119. Gannon, *Florida*. Twenty-two noted historians and anthropologists contributed to this work, the first comprehensive history of the state in twenty-five years. Writing for both lay and scholarly audiences, the authors present not only political, economic, military and religious information but also social history and personal experiences.
120. Handley, Smith and Parker, "Intensive Cultural Resource Assessment Survey," 38–39.
121. Ibid., 85, 87–88.
122. *Spanish Land Grants in Florida*; Handley, Smith and Parker, "Intensive Cultural Resource Assessment Survey," 41.
123. *Caballeria* is an ancient Spanish land tenure similar to the English knight's fee; hence, in Spain and countries settled by the Spanish, a land measure of varying size. In Cuba, it is about 33 acres; in Puerto Rico, about 194 acres; and in the southwestern United States, about 108 acres.
124 . Florida Department of State, Division of library & Information Services. Florida Memory. *The Spanish Archives*. Tallahassee, Florida.
125. Chance and Smith, *Cultural Resource Survey*, 19.
126. *Territory of Florida Map, 1834*, surveyed by Henry Washington, Deputy Surveyor, St. Augustine Historical Society.
127. Weaver, Paul L. *Historic Properties Survey of St. Johns County Florida*. St. Augustine, FL: Historic St. Augustine Preservation Board, September 1985, 68.
128. Chance and Smith, *Cultural Resource Survey*, 20.
129. Weaver, *Historic Properties Survey*.
130. Tebeau, *History of Florida*, 107–9.
131. Handley, Smith and Parker, "Intensive Cultural Resource Assessment Survey," 46.
132. Smith, *Cultural Resource Assessment Survey*.
133. Gannon, *Florida*.
134. Marshall, *This Country of Ours*.
135. Weaver, *Historic Properties Survey*; Tebeau, *History of Florida*; Smith, *Cultural Resource Assessment Survey*; Gannon, *Florida*; Marshall, *This Country of Ours*; Gannon, *New History of Florida*, 157.

Pontevedra, Spain, and Ponte Vedra Beach, Florida

136. Fortes, *El 25 de Julio de 1993*.
137. *Ponte Vedra Recorder*, Friday, May 21, 1971.
138. *Friends Across the Sea*.

THE STOCKTON CONNECTION IN NORTH FLORIDA

139. Personal interview with Jimmy Stockton, 2003; personal interview with Cherie Baker, Stockton Realty Group, Inc., Ponte Vedra Beach, Florida, 2003; phone conversation with Bob Kroner, Stockton Realty, son of Elaine B. Koehl, writer of *The Ponte Vedra Club: The First Fifty-five Years, 1927–1982* and director of publicity and public relations of the Ponte Vedra Club, 1973–82.
140. Randy Noles and Tim Gilmore, "Mineral City Miracle," *Jacksonville* magazine, 1997, 30.
141. Kathy Cramer, "Stockton: 122 Years of One Family's Business," *Ponte Vedra Recorder*, August 31, 2006.
142. *Ponte Vedra Recorder*, "Celebrates Ninetieth Anniversary," December 20, 1974, 3.
143. Ibid.; *Ponte Vedra Recorder*, "The Stocktons' First 100 Years: Jacksonville, Ponte Vedra and the Tomato Plants," November 23, 1984, 15.
144. *Stockton*, 20–21.
145. Jim Terzian, "The Sawgrass Sage: 1972–1982," *Ponte Vedra Recorder*, 1982, 20.
146. *Ponte Vedra Recorder*, August 31, 2006, 1.
147. *Ponte Vedra Recorder*, October 13, 1972, 1.
148. Terzian, "Sawgrass Sage," 27.
149. *Ponte Vedra Recorder*, August 31, 2004.

THE FIRST PONTE VEDRA NEWSPAPERS

150. *Beaches Leader*, 2003.
151. Ibid.

SOUTH PONTE VEDRA BEACH

152. Heilman, "South Ponte Vedra Beach"; personal interview with Inna Heilman, January 26, 2006.
153. Jim and Elaine Dilbeck, "The South Ponte Vedra Group Has Been Active Since '72," *St. Augustine Record*, January 30, 2001.
154. Heilman, "South Ponte Vedra Beach."
155. Neitz, *Cabbageberries, Duck Feathers and the Tides*, 319.
156. *Ponte Vedra Recorder*, "South Ponte Vedra Landmark," March 10, 1972.
157. Susanna Barton, "Condo Sales Clipping Along in South Ponte Vedra Beach," *Jacksonville Business Journal*, July 16, 2001.
158. Heilman, "South Ponte Vedra Beach."
159. Ibid.

VICAR'S LANDING

160. John Searles, "A Life Care Center in Ponte Vedra," *Ponte Vedra Recorder*, December 16, 1983.
161. *Ponte Vedra Recorder*, "Vicar's Landing Life Care Community Planned at Ponte Vedra," June 21, 1985, 5.
162. Robert P.T. Young, "An Opinion," *Ponte Vedra Recorder*, October 25, 1985. Jacksonville Beach Historical Society Archives.

NOCATEE

163. Miranda G. McLeok, "A Tale of Two Counties," *Realty/Builder Connection*, March 2006.

Sources

Adams, Eugene W., DVM, PhD, Professor Emeritus, Tuskegee University. *A Historical Overview of African American Veterinarians in the United States, 1889–2000*. Association of American Medical Colleges (AAVMC), Tuskegee Institute, Alabama.

Adams, William R., PhD. "The King's Road: Florida's First Highway." Florida State Library system under call letters HE356.K564 A373 1997. Unpublished report of construction of Old King's Road in great detail, assisted by Daniel Schafer, Robert Steinbach and Paul Weaver. Written for the City of New Smyrna and Volusia County Board of Commissioners.

American Historical Review 95, no. 1 (n.d.).

Baker, Henry A. Archaeological Excavations at the Shell Bluff Landing Site (8SJ32), St. Johns County, Florida, 1988. Florida Archaeological Reports 5. Bureau of Archaeological Research, Division of Historical Resources, Department of State, Tallahassee.

Bankole, Katheri. *Slavery and Medicine: Enslavement and Medical Practices in Antebellum Louisiana*. Studies in African American History and Culture. New York: Garland Publishing Company, 1998.

Barrows, J., and R. Fingers. "Human Trafficking and the Healthcare Professional." *Southern Medical Journal* 101, no. 5 (May 2008): 464.

Boykin, Sarah Stehlin. *Ponte Vedra Beach: How It Got the Name and the Driving Force Behind the Development of Jacksonillle Beach, 1929–1934*. Atlanta, GA: Beaches Area Historical Society Archives, 1998.

Byrd, W.M. "Race, Medicine, and Health Care in the United States: A Historical Survey." *Southern Journal National Medical Association* EP 34S (2001).

Chance, Marsha A., and Greg C. Smith, Senior Archaeologists. *A Cultural Resource Survey of the Palm Valley Bridge Vicinity*. N.p.: Environmental Services, Inc., June 1992.

Charatz-litt, Cynthia, MPH. "A Chronicle of Racism: The Effects of the White Medical Community on Black Health." *Southern Journal of the National Medical Association* EP 725 (1992). Cedar-Sinai Medical Center, Los Angeles, California.

Colburn, David R., and Jane L. Landers, eds. *The African American Heritage of Florida*. Chapter 2, "Traditions of African American Freedom and Community in Spanish Colonial Florida." Gainesville: University Press of Florida, 1995.

Deagan, Kathleen A. "Fort Mosé: America's First Free Black Community." In *Spanish Pathways in Florida*, edited by Ann L. Henderson and Gary R. Mormino. Sarasota, FL: Pineapple Press, 1991.

———. Phase I Background Research and Assessment of Historic and Prehistoric Archaeological Resources in St. Johns County, 1981. Ms. on file, Historic St. Augustine Preservation Board, St. Augustine, Florida.

Deagan, Kathleen, and Darcie MacMahon. *Fort Mosé: Colonial America's Black Fortress of Freedom.* Gainesville: University Press of Florida, 1995.

De Coste, Frederik. "Suffering of the Shipwrecked Quakers." *True Tales of Old St. Augustine*. St. Petersburg, FL: Great Outdoors Publishing Company, 1966.

Douglas, Andrew E. "A Find of Ceremonial Axes in a Florida Mound." *American Antiquarian* 4 (1882): 100–109.

———. "Some Characteristics of the Indian Earth and Shell Mounds on the Atlantic Coast of Florida." *American Antiquarian* 7 (1885): 74–82, 140–47.

Droz, Robert V. *South Atlantic Coastal Highway* map. *Florida Auto Trails.* Mulberry, FL: Dave Schul Site, 2001. Library of Congress Archives.

Droz, Robert V., with Hollis L. Carroll, contr. *Florida Auto Trails*. Tallahassee: Florida Department of Transportation, 2001.

Fortes, Xose. *El 25 de Julio de 1993. Galicia y el mar. Este Libro Se Termino de Imprimar and La Ria de Pontevedra. El Dia 26 de Setiembre de 1986. Centenario del Puerto de Marin 1886–1986*. St. Johns County Library, Ponte Vedra Beach, Florida.

Fort Mosé: A New Chapter in American History, video, 1993. Ironwood Productions, Winter Park, Florida.

Franklin, John Hope, and Alfred A. Moss Jr. *From Slavery to Freedom*. Columbus, OH: McGraw Hill Publishing, 1988.

Gannon, Michael V. *Florida: A Short History*. Gainesville: University Press of Florida, 1993.

Green-McKenzie, J. "Training African-American Residents in the 20th Century." *Southern Journal of the National Medical Association* (2004).

Griffin, Patricia C. "Life on the Plantations of East Florida 1763–1848." *Florida Anthropologist* 56, no. 3 (September 2003): 163–88.

Guana Tolomato Matanzas National Estuarine Research Reserve Management Plan, December 2008. Florida Department of Environmental Protection Coastal and Aquatic Managed Areas, Tallahassee, Florida.

Hagy, J.W. "International Conference on Biomedical Horizons of the Leech." *Southern Blood Coagulation and Fibrinolysis* EP 68 (1990).

Halperin, E.C. "The Poor, the Black, and the Marginalized as the Source of Cadavers in the United States Anatomical Education." *Southern Clinical Anatomy* EP495 (2007).

Handley, Brent, Greg Smith and Susan Parker. "An Intensive Cultural Resource Assessment Survey of the Nocatee Tract, Duval and St. Johns Counties, Florida." Unpublished manuscript, Jacksonville, Florida. 2000.

Hann, John H. *A History of Timucua Indians and Missions*. Ripley P. Bullen Series. Gainesville: Florida Museum of Natural History, 1996.

———. "Summary Guide to Spanish Florida Missions and Visitas with Churches in the Sixteenth and Seventeenth Centuries." *The Americas* 46 (1990): 417–513.

Harley, Sharon. *The Timetables of African-American History: A Chronology of the Most Important People and Events in African-American History*. New York: Simon & Schuster, 1995.

Harvey, Karen G. *America's First City: St. Augustine's Historic Neighborhoods*. N.p.: Tailored Tours, 1997.

Heilman, Inna. "South Ponte Vedra Beach: Why It Is a Special Place to Live," 1989. University of North Florida Library, Special Collection, Jacksonville, Florida.

Jonathan Dickenson's Journey, 1696–1697. Florida Heritage Collection. London: printed and sold by James Phillips, 1787. Located at the Florida State Library, Tallahassee.

Jones, Maxine K., and Kevin M. McCarthy. *African Americans in Florida*. Tallahassee: Florida State University, 1993.

Jones, Norrece T., Jr. *Born a Child of Freedom Yet a Slave*. Lebanon, NH: University Press of New England, 1990.

Kenny, S.C. "'I Can Do the Child No Good': Dr. Sims and the Enslaved Infants of Montgomery, Alabama." *Southern Social History of Medicine* EP 241 (2007).

Landers, Jane. "Free and Slave." In *The New History of Florida*, edited by Michael Gannon. Gainesville, FL: University Press of Florida, 1996.

———. "Gracia Real de Santa Teresa de Mosé: A Free Black Town in Spanish Colonial Florida." *El Escribano* 28 (1991).

———. "Mosé." *American Historical Review* 95, no. 1 (n.d.).

———. "The Mose Site." *El Escribano* 10 (April 1973).

Lander, K., and J. Pritchett. "When to Care: The Economic Rationale of Slavery Health Care Provision." *Southern Social Science History* (2009).

Lumb, Robin. *Stockton: A Tradition in Real Estate Since 1884*. Jacksonville, FL: Simons Media Services for Stockton Real Estate, 2004.

Marshall, Henrietta Elizabeth. *This Country of Ours: The Story of the United States*. New York: George H. Doran Company, 1917.

McCarthy, Kevin M. *Black Florida*. Chapter 58. N.p.: Hippocrene Books, 1995.

McGoun, William E. *Southeast Florida Pioneers: The Palm and Treasure Coast*. Sarasota, FL: Pineapple Press, 1998.

Melching, Stephen D., President, Friends Across the Sea. *Friends Across the Sea: The Pontevedra/Ponte Vedra Beach Connection*. Ponte Vedra Beach, FL: JCJ Publishing, 2002.

Miller, James L. *An Environmental History of Northeast Florida*. Gainesville: University Press of Florida, 1998.

Morgan, T.M. "The Education and Medical Practice of Dr. James McCune Smith (1813–1865), First Black American to Hold a Medical Degree." *Southern Journal of the National Medical Association* (2003).

Neitz, Grahl Barkoskie. *Cabbageberries, Duck Feathers and the Tides: A Collection of Palm Valley Memories.* Flagler Beach, FL: Ocean Publishing, 2006.

The New History of Florida. Gainesville: University Press of Florida, 1996.

Nolan, Hamilton. "White Man's Burden: How an Unapologetic Good Ol' Boy Became the Savior of Black History in St. Augustine." *Folioweekly*, 2003.

O'Sullivan, Maurice, and Jack C. Lane. *Jonathan Dickenson in the Florida Reader: Visions of Paradise from 1530 to the Present.* Sarasota, FL: Pineapple Press, 1991.

Painter, Nell Irvin. *Sojourner Truth: A Life, a Symbol.* New York: W.W. Norton, 1996.

Parker, Susan R. Documentation for the Shell Bluff National Register Nomination, 1991. Ms. on file, CARL Project, St. Augustine, Florida.

Porter, Kenneth. "Negroes on the Southern Frontier, 1670–1763." *Journal of Negro History* 53 (January 1948): 53–78. Cited in *The Underground Railroad in American History* by the National Park Service.

Rivers, Larry Eugene. *Slavery in Florida: Territorial Days to Emancipation.* Gainesville: University Press of Florida, 2000.

Ryan, William P. *The Search for Old King's Road: The First Route into Florida.* Flagler Beach, FL: Old Kings Road Press, 2006.

Schafer, Daniel L. "Early Plantation Development in British East Florida." *El Escribano* 19, no. 37 (1982): 47. James Grant to Richard Oswald, Bound Letter Book, August 31, 1766, and October 12, 1765. Ballindalloch Castle Muniments.

———. "Governor James Grant's Villa: A British East Florida Indigo Plantation." *El Escribano* (2000): 90.

———. *The Oldest City: St. Augustine Saga of Survival.* St. Augustine, FL: St. Augustine Historical Society, 1983.

———. "Yellow Silk Ferret Tied Round Their Wrist: African Americans in British East Florida, 1873–1784." In *The African American Heritage of Florida*, edited by David R. Colburn and Jane L. Landers. Gainesville: University Press of Florida, 1995.

Smith, Greg C. *A Cultural Resource Assessment Survey of the Sanchez Grant Tracts and Plantation Annex St. Johns County, Florida*, June 1992. Environmental Services, Inc., Jacksonville, Florida.

Spanish Land Grants in Florida. Brief Translations from the Archives of the Boards of Commissioners for Ascertaining Claims and Titles to Land in the Territory of Florida. Vols. 1, 3 and 4. Prepared by the Historical Records Survey Division of Community Service Programs, Work Projects Administration. Tallahassee, FL: State Library Board, 1941.

Tebeau, Charles. *A History of Florida.* Coral Gables: University of Miami Press, 1971.

Tyson, Timothy B. *Blood Done Sign My Name.* New York: Three Rivers Press, 2004.

Voyages Database. "The Trans-Atlantic Slave Trade Database: Assessing the Slave Trade," Emory University, 2009.

Wall, L.L. "The Medical Ethics of Dr. J. Marion Sims: A Fresh Look at the Historical Record." *Southern Journal of Medical Ethics* EP 350 (2006).

Watts, Rosalyn J. "Race Consciousness and the Health of African Americans." *Southern Online Journal of Issues in Nursing* 8, no. 1, manuscript 3 (2003).

Weaver, Paul L. *Historic Properties Survey of St. Johns County Florida.* St. Augustine, FL: Historic St. Augustine Preservation Board, September 1985.

Weisman, Brent R., and Christine Newman. Draft National Register of Historic Places Registration Form, Wright's Landing (SJ3), 1992. Ms. on file, CARL Project Office, St. Augustine, Florida.

West, Jean M. *Archaeology of Early Colonial Life: Slavery and Sanctuary in Colonial Florida.* Peterborough, NH: Cobblestone Publishing Company, 1998.

William Mayo Fulton's letterbook, 1837–44. Virginia Historical Society Archives, Richmond, Virginia, Mss5:2F959:1.

Wilson, Gil. *Dr. Bronson and Friends: A History of the City of St. Augustine,* Laudator temporis acti *(One who praises past times).* St. Augustine, FL: St. Augustine Historical Society, 2006.

Windley, Lathan Algerna. "A Profile of Runaway Slaves in Virginia and South Carolina from 1730 through 1787." In *Studies in African American History and Culture,* edited by Graham Hodges. New York: Garland Publishing Company, 1995.

Worth, John. "Tolomato in the Documentary Record: An Overview." Ms. on file, CARL Project, St. Augustine, Florida.

Wright, Irene J. "Dispatches of Spanish Officials Bearing on the Free Negro Settlement of Gracia Real de Santa Teresa de Mosé, Florida." *Journal of Negro History* (April 1924).

About the Author and the Artist

Maurice Robinson was transferred from Richmond, Virginia, to Ponte Vedra Beach, Florida, in 1993 as an accountant with CSX Corporation. He retired in 2003 after thirty-five years. Born in Virginia, he holds a bachelor's degree from Virginia Commonwealth University and has completed classes at the University of North Florida. His interests focus on north Florida and especially the "First Coast" topics in St. Johns County, Florida. He now resides with his wife in historic Midlothian, Virginia. See more information at jacksonvillemiracleman.wordpress.com

Ellen Diamond, whose painting appears on the cover, is a resident of Ponte Vedra Beach. She is an internationally acclaimed contemporary impressionist whose subjects range from the local beaches and marshes of northern Florida to the landscapes of Tuscany and Provence, both of which she visits regularly. See more information at ellendiamond.com